Case Studies with the Constitution of the Republic of Korea

내일을여는지식 법 20

EDITOR PROF. DR. IUR. PARK, KYU HWAN

Case Studies with the Constitution of the Republic of Korea

한국학술정보㈜

The LORD is my shepherd,
I shall not be in want.
(Psalms 23:1)

ACKNOWLEDGMENTS

Heaven helps those who help themselves.

This book, completed by the students' devotion, is a work of passion. I appreciate what students had done in trust and would especially like to thank all students with giving respect. At the last class, we talked about precious worth that we feel in our life.

TRUST, LOVE, JUSTICE, STUDY, JESUS, HUMAN, CAREER, PASSION, FAMILY, SINCERITY, HOPE, ATTRACTIVE, COURAGE, MIRACLE.

I believe these kinds of dreams are realized in the near future with the help from heaven. I pray for and hope to be.

Kyu-hwan Park
Editor
The college of Law, Youngsan University

Vorwort des Herausgebers

(Dieses Buch ist) Ein großes Wundergeschenk! Denn ich zweifelte selber, ob alle Studenten bei meiner Englisch Vorlesung weiter bleiben können oder möchten. Aber, erkenntlich, ich kann und darf auf meine Jünger, die vor der unglaubigen Leidenschaft explodiert waren, sehr stolz sein. Ja! Du geschafft!

Es ist bemerkenswert, unter welchen Umständen "Case studies with the Constitution of the Republic of Korea" entstand ist. Am Anfang dieser Vorlesung hatte fast alle Studenten Angst gegen die rechtswissenschaftliche Englisch Literatur und deshalb sollte schon ein Student sie aufgeben. Aber allmählich, entsprechend ihren geschafften Präsentationen, hielt und gefühlte die Teilnehmer Selbstvertrauen. Endlich, auf Grund von ihrer Mühe, lassen sie sich freigeben von der schwierigen, – ein Semester dauer und nur Englisch benutzen durfte – aber freiwilligen sog. Gefängnisklasse. Es ist großer Erfolg für uns alle. Ich hoffe aufrichtig und ehrlich, dass meine Begleitung und dieses Buch eine wundervolle Hoffnungsbasis für die Leben meiner Studenten werden dürfen, wie meine verehrten Lehrer Prof. Dr. iur. Sung – Soo Kim an der Yonsei Universität in Korea, Prof. Dr. iur. Michael Kilian an der Matin – Luther Universität Halle – Wittenberg in Deutschland mir gegeben hatten.

Und auch besonders habe ich Präsident Dr. Gu – wuck Bu an der Youngsan Universität zu verdanken, weil mir seine Ermutigung, auf der ich English Vorlesung halten konnte, eine tiefe reine Quelle gewesen wurde.

Kyu – hwan Park

Preface

This book is an collection of English reports for the cases of Korean Constitutional Court in the class of Practical Studies of Constitution. It's been 4 months since this class first started. All of students have studied the essential cases of the Constitutional Court. We all might had suffered from experiencing English all over the textbook and having presentation only in English during the class. Each student studied allotted case by themselves and gave a speech before our professor and other students almost every week.

At the first time of English presentation, we all had slight doubts whether we could possibly accomplish our works, and felt a little bit of shame and worries as well. However, as time goes, the more cases were presented, the better we got attitude toward it. We started to feel fruitful, and excited. Finally, yes, we finished our real challenging studies. Now we feel very proud of ourselves to make a challenge, not to avoid. It was clearly a great opportunity that we could study the Constitution and English at the same time.

Our the Jesus man professor Park Kyu hwan, we all appreciate what you've done in and out of the class. A great class leader, Kim Eun ho, and other classmates, Kim Kun young, Park Jin a, Park Hye ju, Lee Su rim, Lee Su jeen, Lee Hyun ho, Cheong Han sae beol. The atmosphere of our class was incredible, too. Warm and good people gathered all together. Here is a small result of our efforts. We consider this one little book could be an example of class studies.

Well done guys, There's laid a bright future for us.

Constitution study team

contents

CASE 1

The Act on Special Cases concerning Expedition, etc. of Legal Proceedings case[1)]
(소송촉진등에관한특례법 제6조의 위헌심판제청)
88Hun-Ka7, January 25, 1989

A. Summary of the case

The Court delivered its first en banc unconstitutionality decision in this case. The Court struck down the proviso of Article 6 (1) of the Act on Special Cases concerning Expedition, etc. of Legal Proceedings which grants the state a superior legal status of being immune from provisional execution. This decision is the first decision of the Court after its inception and also its first decision of unconstitutionality. And it as turning point in our state-centered way of thinking in making and enforcing of the laws.

B. Issue of the case

1) Rules of the trial whether to admit(accept) Constitution of the Korea Preamble ?

---

1) The Constitutioanl Court of Korea, The First Ten Years of the Korean Constitutioanl Court (1988~1998), 2001, 186ff.

- Negative effect : Not admit
- Affirmative effect : Admit

Institutions of the country and citizens must respect and obey the best value. Therefore, Constitution of the Korea Preamble rules of the trial Legal effect will be recognized.

2) The proviso of Article 6 (1) of the Act whether a violation of the Constitution ?

- Principle of equality
- Operation of the national treasury

Since the principle of equality rightly applies to "the property rights of the people" guaranteed by Article 23 and the "right to speedy trial" guaranteed by Article 27 (3) of the Constitution, no party should be discriminated based on his identity in civil proceedings on private rights such as property rights. Even the state should not be favored without reasonable basis. This is because, in a civil suit on the legal relations formed by operation of the national treasury, not by exercise of the state power, the state must be treated the same as a private person.

An order of provisional execution deters unnecessary abuses of appeals and allows expedited enforcement of rights, thereby protecting his or her property right and right to speedy trial. Article 6 (1) of the Act mandates granting an order of provisional execution to the prevailing state but prohibits such order for a prevailing private person no matter how convincing his or her judgment is. The provision therefore discriminates against parties in protecting property rights and rights to speedy trials, and such discrimination is without reasonable cause.

C. Personal opinion (Lee, Su-rim)

The principle of equality is the supreme principle in the field of protection of basic rights. It provides a standard which the state must abide by in interpreting or executing laws and mandate on the state not to discriminate without reasonable cause. It is everyone's right and the most basic of all basic rights. So depending on the principle of equality, I agree that the decision (the proviso Article 6 (1) of the Act on Special Cases concerning Expedition, etc. of Legal Proceedings which grants the state a superior legal status of being immune from provisional execution) is in violation of the Constitution.

CASE 2

Deeming Title Trust as Gift case[2]
(상속세법 제32조의2의 위헌여부에 관한 헌법소원)
89Hun-Ma38, July 21, 1989

A. Summary of the case

The claimant was the president of Seoul Petroleum Company which was in the process of purchasing some land. According to the claimant, because he had difficulty obtaining the certificate of farmland sales and the seller was unwilling to transfer the ownership registration to the Company, he had the title transferred to himself and later to the company.

However, the Director of Yongsan Tax Office deemed the initial purchase under the claimant's name as a gift to the claimant pursuant to the Inheritance Tax Act, and levied a gift tax. At the Seoul High Court, the claimant sued the director for nullification of the levy, arguing that taxation on pseudo gift is illegal. He lost and appealed to the Supreme Court; when his motion for constitutional review of the Inheritance Tax Act was turned down, he also filed a constitutional complaint.

* The Inheritance Tax Act : deems the properties, that are subject to

---

2) Ibid., 189ff.

compulsory registration, gifted the recorded owner even if another person is the equitable owner. the Inheritance Tax Act states that, as to the property subject to compulsory recording, registration or renewal for all transfers of its rights.

B. Issue of the law

Constitutional review of the Inheritance Tax Act

The Inheritance Tax should be interpreted to deem the properties subject to compulsory recording to have been gifted to the recorded owner on the day of recording, except in an exceptional situation where registering under the real owner was impracticable due to restrictions in other positive laws or a third party's non-cooperation. It has limited constitutionality only under such interpretation.

C. Personal opinion (Park, Hye-ju)

This decision was reported as the Court's acceptance of a view that property rights were being infringed under the pretext of increasing tax revenue and facilitating fiscal administration, and also as the Court's first check on indiscriminate impositirst chng tax res even on inevitable title trusts without any evasive purpose.

I dissent from majority opinion, finding violation of Articles 38 and 59 of the Constitution which prescribe the principle of statutory taxation.

* Article 38 : All citizens shall have the duty to pay
   taxes under the conditions as prescribed by Act.
* Article 59 : Types and rates of taxes shallbe determined by Act.

CASE 3

Forests Survey Inspection Request case[3]
(공권력에 의한 재산권침해에 대한 헌법소원)
88Hun-Ma22, September 4, 1989

A. Summary of the case

1) In order to recover the title to the land, he repeatedly requested the respondent Supervisor of County of Ichon of the Kyong-ki Do (Province) for inspection and duplication of the documents. The respondent did not take any action on the land surveys and private forests use surveys.

2) He thought that there is a hindrance to property right recovery. So he requisitioned a constitutional petition judgment in 1988. 12. 17.

3) It seems that noncompliance of the government is not his property right infringement. But there is no reason for insisting non-disclosure of the requested documents themselves, or statutes or regulations. Therefore, the government's inaction on the complainant's request breached his right to know.

4) His unfounded allegation requested for inspection and duplication of the old forests title records and land tax ledgers. Therefore this case decision is rejection.

---

3) Ibid., 132ff.

B. Issue of the law

1) Inaction or action of respondent about his inspection and duplication of the documents.

2) Infringe the fundamental right of the applicant, yes or no.

C. Personal opinion (Kim, Eun–ho)

I agree to this judgment. It seems that noncompliance of the government is not his property right infringement. But Infringed his right to know. His requested for inspection and duplication of the documents is supporting evidence. Therefore It seems that not his recover the title to the land. Also do not be able to judge about his proprietary right. So it is difficult to property right infringement. But there is no reason for insisting non-disclosure of the requested documents themselves, or statutes or regulations. Therefore, the government's inaction on the complainant's request breached his right to know.

National Assembly Candidacy Deposit case[4)]
(국회의원선거법 제33조 제34조의 위헌심판제청)
88Hun-Ka6, September 8, 1989

A. Summary of the case

The court found non-conforming to the Constitution Article 33 and 34 of the Election of National Assembly Members Act(hereafter 'the Act').

Article 33 (1) of the Act requires independent candidates to make a deposit of twenty million won to the local Election Commission at the time of registering as a candidate and party nominees to deposit ten million won. Article 34 then forfeits the deposits minus some expenses in the event that the candidate resigns, nullifies his registration, or failures to gain one-third of the effective votes.

B. Issue of the law

The deposit requirement of ten or twenty million is prohibitive to people of ordinary income or in their twenties' or thirties', and therefore

---

4) Ibid., 172ff.

permits only the wealthy to the candidacy. They violate the basic principles of people's sovereignty and of free democracy in relation to right of equality (Article 11), right to vote (Article 24) and right to hold public office (Article 25) of the Constitution. The role of political parties is indispensable to democratic polity. but, the deposit requirement for independent candidates amounting to twice the amount required of party nominees gives the independent candidates substantial competitive disadvantages and suppress their candidacy. so, it violates the principles of equal election (Article 41) and of equality (Article 11) of the Constitution.

Forfeiting the deposits from the candidates who fail to gain on-third of the effective votes is too stringent and unprecedented in comparative-legal perspectives. It violates Article 116 (2) to the candidates. However, having respect for the authority of the legislature and the homogeneity of its membership, the national assembly must do the revisions themselves; the Court hereby finds the Act non-conforming to the Constitution.

C. Personal opinion (Lee, Hyun-Ho)

Why the deposits system is suggested that non-conforming Constitution? I think that Article 33 and 34 of the Election of National Assembly Members Act is not a problem of the deposit system but an amount of the deposit is too large that gives rise to encroach people's right to vote consequently. so that it incur bad result which encroach an election system of substance and foundation of democratic form of government. In accordance with this, it violates the right of equality (Article 11), right to vote (Article 24) and right to hold public office (Article 25) the principles of equal election (Article 41) and of equality (Article 11) and Article 116 (2) of the Constitution.

Praising and Encouraging under National Security Act case[5]
(국가보안법 제7조에 대한 위헌심판)
89Hun-Ka113, April 2, 1990

A. Summary of the case

The problematic statute was enacted to protect national security and people's liberties from the threat of anti-state activities under looming possibility of the North-South military confrontation. The petitioners were prosecuted and tried for possessing and distributing books and other expressive materials for the purpose of benefiting an antistate organization under Article 7 (1) and (5) of the National Security Act. They made motion for constitutional review of the said statute and the presiding court granted the motion. The court in this case reviewed Article 7(1) and (5) found it constitutional only as it applies to the limited circumstances threatening national security and the basic order of free democracy.

B. Issue of the law

1) vague terms – the expressions such as "member", "activities", "sympa-

---

5) Ibid., 134ff.

thizes", or "benefits" are too vague for ordinary people to have a reasonable standard to determine the contents and boundaries of their definition – suppress freedom of expression, freedom of speech, press, and principle of rule of law, and statutory punishment.

2) not consistent with the preamble to the Constitution – unity of the Korean race through justice, humanity, and national brotherhood pursuant to the mandate of peaceful unification- & Article 4-peaceful unification

3) interpretation should make provision consistent with the constitution and avoid unconstitutional interpretation of terms and give positive aspects- Article 7 (1) and (5) are not un constitutional as it is narrowly interpreted to cover only those activities posing a clear threat to the integrity and the security of the nation and the basic order of free democracy.

4) minority opinion – law so clearly unconstitutional cannot be cured merely by interpreting it narrowly and should simply be stricken down.

C. Personal opinion (Park, Jin–a)

In my opinion, terms of previous statute like "member" or "sympathizes" have possibility of including innocent people who consider North Korea as brotherhood concept due to the vague and broad meanings that can be interpreted into various ways. In this situation, it could permit the law enforcement agencies to arbitrarily enforce the law. Even though problematic expressions had been amended into certain terms after this case, under the liberal democracy, this statute basically and potentially suppress the fundamental rights such as free of speech and press. Furthermore, Nation exists fully by the citizens which mean national security is the means of their right to pursue happiness.

CASE 6

Adultery case[6)
(형법 제241조의 위헌여부에 관한 헌법소원)
89Hun–Ma82, September 10, 1990

A. Summary of the case

The complainant was charged with adultery and sentenced to one year in prison at the first trial and to eight months by the appellate court. Upon appeal of the conviction to the Supreme Court, he requested constitutional review of Article 241 of the Criminal Act outlawing adultery. When the Supreme Court denied the motion, the complainant filed a constitutional complaint with the Constitutional Court.

B. Issue of the law

Judging the relationship between the right to sexual self-determination and the crime of adultery, the Constitutional Court upheld Article 241 of the Criminal Act on adultery.

1) Article 241 of the Criminal Act is aimed at maintaining sexual morality and the monogamous conjugal system, protecting sexual fidelity

---

6) Ibid., 235ff.

between husbands and wives, guaranteeing a family life, and deterring social evils arising from adultery. To that end, it bans adultery by a married person and subjects the transgressors to a punishment of up to two years of incarceration. They constitute a necessary minimum regulation on sexual self-determination and do not violate the rule against excessive restriction and the rule against violation of the essence of basic constitutional rights.

2) The adultery provision is not in violation of Article 36 (1) of the Constitution, the provision is consistent with the constitutional duty of the state to guarantee marriage and family life on the basis of individual dignity and gender equality. The provision does not violate the principle of equality.

* Article 36 (1) : Marriage and family life should be based on and maintained by individual dignity and gender equality, and the state shall guarantee this institution.

C. Personal opinion (Park, Hye-ju)

I dissent from majority opinion.

1) On matters of sexual self-determination, Article 10 of the Constitution on the right of personality and the right to pursue happiness presumes the individual right to self-determination, which includes right to sexual self-determination, namely, right to decide whether and with whom to enter into sexual relationships.

* Article 10 : All citizens shall be assured of human dignity and worth and have the right to pursue happiness. It shall be the duty of the State to confirm and guarantee the fundamental and inviolable human rights of individuals.

2) Criminal punishment for adultery itself was constitutional, but the

adultery provision provides incarceration as the only form of punishment without allowing more moderate forms of penalty, and is therefore unconstitutional.

3) Stating that the adultery prohibition was unconstitutional as a violation of right to withhold private matter from disclosure or of the principle against excessive restriction.

Rule implementing the Certified Judicial Scriveners Act case[7)]

(법무사법시행규칙에 대한 헌법소원)

89Hun—Ma178, October 15, 1990

A. Summary of the case

Article 4 of the Certified Judicial Scrivener Act grants a judicial scrivener's license, firstly, to a person with seven or more tears of experience in the ordinary courts, the Constitutional Court, or the prosecutor's offices as an administrator or a higher position, who had been certified by the chief justice of the supreme court as having necessary legal knowledge and ability to carry out the tasks of a certified judicial scrivener; thirdly, to a person who passed the judicial scrivener's license examination (Section 1). Section 2 of the provision delegates matters concerning certification and exam administration to be determined by the Rules of the Supreme Court. However, Article 3 (1) of the Rules authorized by the above provisions, states "the Minister of Court Administration may administer the examination upon approval from the Chief Justice of the Supreme Court when he recognizes need for additional judicial scriveners" The complainant worked as a clerk in a judicial scrivener's office and was preparing to take the examination.

---

7) Ibid., 194ff.

he filed a contravenes Article 4(1) (ii) intended to administer the exam regularly, and leaves to the discretion of the Minister of Court Administration wether the exam is Administered. The complaint asserts that Article 3 (1) of the Rules took away his opportunity to take the examination and thus violated his right of equality.

B. Issue of the law

The Court struck down Article 3 (1) of the Rules implementing the Certified Judicial Scriveners Act for violating right of equality(Article 11(1) of the Constitution) and the freedom to choose one's own occupation(Article 15 of the Constitution)

C. Personal opinion (Lee, Hyun-ho)

Article 3(1) of the Rules implementing the Certified Judicial Scriveners Act is non-constitution. Because PREAMBLE of the Constitution states "To afford equal opportunities to every person and provide for the fullest development of individual capabilities in all fields, including political, economic, social and cultural life...". And Article 11(1) of the Constitution states "All citizens shall be equal before the law" which mandates equality of opportunity and principle of equality. And it also violates the freedom to choose one's own occupation(Article 15 of the Constitution). Therefore, Article 3 (1) of the Rules implementing the Certified Judicial Scriveners Act should be reversed by Article 75 (3) of the Constitutional Court Act.

Notice of Apology case[8]
(민법 제764조 위헌여부에 관한 헌법소원)
89Hun—Ma160, April 1, 1991

A. Summary of the case

The plaintiff, a former Miss Korea 김○○ bring a suit against ○○ 일보. Because Her defamation of character. She was based on Article 764 of Civil Act. Her demand an apology of notice.

However, this decision is unconstitutional. Notice of Apology' violation of constitutional because freedom of conscience and freedom of silence.

Constitutional Court dismissed ○○일보's unconstitutional about 'notice of apology'. Article 764 of Civil Act does not represented notice of apology. So, Article 764 of Civil Act dose not mean unconstitutional.

B. Issue of the law

Constitutional Court about 'Notice of apology' decision as below. A fact, defamation of character restored notice of apology general opinion. But, there is limit in press and publication. Therefore, notice of apology

---

8) Ibid., 138ff.

need for society.

It infringes basis right to require notice of apology not to think that individual committed mistake. That violated freedom of conscience and freedom of silence. An apology should does voluntarily. Notice of apology was compelled by law. This violated personal right.

Fundamental right violated under the pressure of 'Notice of apology'. The other way find that does not violated freedom of conscience. For example, cancel of notice, insert an case(a written judgment) in a newspaper or magazine. In this case, Constitutional Court was narrowly focused on Article 764 of Civil Act.

C. Personal opinion (Lee, Soo-jeen)

I agree with the Constitutional Court decision. Because defamation of character dose not compelled by law. It was violated of fundamental right. You should apology does voluntarily. Freedom of conscience, freedom of silence is our personal right. I think that like cancel of notice, insert written judgement an newspaper.

Prescriptive Acquisition of Miscellaneous State Property case[9)]

(국유재산법 제5조 제2항에 관한 위헌심판)

89Hun-Ka97, May 13, 1991

A. Summary of the case

Since 1961, the claimant has occupied and managed a tract of forest located in Kyunggi Yichun County. The state recorded preservation of the title on the property in 1987. The claimant sued the state at the Suwon District Court, demanding cancellation of the recording on the basis of time bar, and requested constitutional review of Article 5 (2) of the State Properties Act, challeng of miscellaneous properties as being violative of Article 11 (1) right to equality and Article 23 (1) right to property. The Suwon District Court granted the motion and referred the case to the Constitutional Court for review.

B. Issue of the law

1) Chariteristics of miscellaneous property.

National property is classified into three kinds according to its purpose ;

---

9) Ibid., 198ff.

administrative property, preservation property, miscellaneous property.

Unlike administrative property or preservation property, miscellaneous property is subject to purchase, lease, and other private transactions governed by general principles of private economic order in accordance with its economic value. In the case of miscellaneous property, the state has rights as a corporation in equal legal relations with private persons in which its action and the changes in rights are given effects. The state is in principle subject to private law.

2) Whether or not the ban on prescriptive acquisition is unconstitutional.

The state's act of lending or selling miscellaneous property is a private act carried out by a private economic actor, and its legal relations are private legal relations subject to private laws. Therefore, just as the state may acquire a private person's property by operation of time bar, the private person must be able to do the same to the state. under Article 5 (2), miscellaneous property is included in state properties exempt from prescriptive acquisition. It is a fundamental constitutional principle that there should not be any discrimination based on the party's identity in legal relations governing private rights. Even the state must be treated equally in relation to private persons when it comes to private relations created by operation of the national treasury. The provision violates these principles.

C. Personal opinion (Cheong, Han—sae—beol)

Basically, state-owned property must be reserved for welfare of the entire people. Exempting it from time bar acquisition is necessary in order to promote efficiency of land management and to prevent its erosion through privatization. Therefore, the provision which made a denial of prescriptive acquisition on national property to achieve a legislative purpose of preventing the erosion through the privatization of national property can be justifiable. I agree with Justices Cho yu-kwang, Byun Jeong-soo and Kim Yang-kyun on that point.

Mandatory Fire Insurance case[10)]
(화재로인한재해보상과보험가입에관한법률 제5조 제1항의
위헌여부에 관한 헌법소원)
89Hun-Ma204, June 3, 1991

A. Summary of the case

The complainant, who owns four-storied building, has paid a premium on fire insurance for this building purchased from Korean Fire Protection Association who have signed the Agreement for Joint Underwriting of Liability Insurance. He sued, demanding reimbursement of the premium, and requested constitutional review of the above provision. Upon denial, he filed a constitutional complaint.

B. Issue of the law

The court ruled, that inclusion of "four- or more story building" under the "special building" category of Article 5 of the Act on the Indemnification for Fire-Caused Loss and the Purchase of Insurance Policies is partially unconstitutional.

Freedom of contract includes freedom not to form a contract, meaning

---

10) Ibid., 200ff.

that one should not be forced into an undesired contract by law or state. It is derived from the general freedom of action implied in the right to pursue happiness of article 10 of the Constitution.

The contract of this case restricts both freedom of contract and general freedom of action. Therefore, it violates the principles concerning limitation on basic rights.

C. Personal opinion (Kim, Eun-ho)

The freedom of contract is included in the general freedom of action as part of the constitutional right to pursue happiness. Therefore this must be guaranteed in basic right. There is dissent. But I think that the restrict for article 37 clause 2 is not included.

Request for a Corrective Report case[11]

(정기간행물의등록등에관한법률 제19조 제3항, 제16조 제3항의
위헌여부에 관한 헌법소원)

89Hun-Ma165, September 16, 1991

A. Summary of the case

The JoongAng Ilbo, published by the complainant, was sued by the Pasteur Dairy corporation in the Seoul District Civil Court for a July 23, 1988 story concerning Pasteur Dairy which appeared in its Reporter's Notepad section.

The JoongAng Ilbo was ordered to print a corrective material when Pasteur Dairy prevailed in the action for a corrective report pursuant to the above statute. The complainant moved for constitutional review of the statute for infringing freedom of press and the press' right to trial, and when denied, brought a constitutional complaint.

B. Issue of the law

The basic rights of the contention : Right to reply as request for a Corrective Report VS freedom of the press.

---

11) Ibid., 140ff.

A right to reply protect to men's right to personality such a right is derived from the general right to personality, right to privacy, freedom of privacy guaranteed by the constitution.

But this Act impose indirect limitations on reporting, and therefore should adhere to the rule against excessive restriction so that all rights complementing freedom of press are given the maximum effects.

In short, the challenged Law achieves a well-struck balance between the two conflicting interest.

* Reference details : In Periodicals Act, a definition of the word "correction" means a right to request that the reporting agency publish rebuttal by those affected by the report. Hence, right to reply. Reply does not aim to contest the truth of the report or compel correction of a false report. After this case, the National Assembly revised the Act (Act. 5145) on December 30, 1995 to reconcile it with the decision, inter alia replacing 'right to a corrective report' with 'right to reply'.

C. Personal opinion (Park, Hye-ju)

There are lots of basic rights of the contention. All basic rights aren't satisfied. On this case was appraised as a great achievement for clearly stating that the conflicts between basic rights should be resolved by harmonizing competing provisions pursuant to the uniformity of the Constitution and also for emphasizing the meaning and function of freedom of press as an objective normative order.

Military Secret Leakage case[12)]
(군사기밀보호법 제6조 등에 관한 위헌심판)
89Hun-Ka104, February 25, 1992

A. Summary of the case

The article 6, 7 and 10 of the Military Secret Protection Act (hereinafter MSPA) provides punishment for "detection and collection of military secrets through inappropriate means (Article 6)," "leakage of military secrets by those who dejects and collects them (Article 7)," and "leakage of military secrets by those who obtained or possessed them accidentally (Article 10)." The concepts of 'military secrets' and 'inappropriate means' were criticized for being so vague that the provisions that included them violated the rule of clarity of law and the essential content of right to know.

B. Issue of the law

The court conclude the Articles 6, 7 and 10 of MSPA on limited constitutionality after explaining the relationship between the military

---

12) Ibid., 142ff.

secrets and the principle of statutory punishment.

1) no violation of the rule of clarity required by the principle of statutory punishment.

2) "detection and collection through inappropriate means (Article 6)" is sufficiently clear to those with ordinary sensibilities; therefore, it does not violate of the rule of clarity of law, either.

3) 'military secrets' in Article 6, 7 and 10 of MSPA shoud be interpreted narrowly to mean only the undisclosed facts classified and marked through proper procedures, the contents of which will, upon leakage, pose a clear threat to national security due to their confidential nature.

C. Personal opinion (Lee, Hyun-ho)

To clear the law requisite, it means that lawmaker's legislation intention can be understood generally by healthful common sense people, In the law.

even if it use and stipulate a general idea which needs a judge's supplementary analysis in the somewhat large extent and some about limits, it because doesn't violate definition rule if it is analyzed diverse meaningly in the application phase, the concept of "military secrets" cannot be violated definition rule.

In the MSPA provides punishment for "detection and collection of military secrets through inappropriate means (Article 6), the concepts of 'inappropriate means' cannot violate definition rule and concreteness because the concept cannot too vague or too large extent and sufficiently identify or foresee.

Periodicals Registration case[13]
(정기간행물의등록등에관한법률 제7조 제1항의 위헌심판)
90Hun-Ka23, June 26, 1992

A. Summary of the case

This case inquired whether Article 7 (1) of the Registration, etc. of Periodicals Act (hereinafter RPA), which requires all periodicals to be registered for publication violates the ban on licensing of publication in Article 21 (2) of the constitution. The case was resolved on a decision of limited unconstitutionality.

The complainants were being prosecuted at the Seoul District Criminal Court pursuant to RPA for having published "Chunminrun Shinmun" twice a month from March 10 to June 25, 1989, eight times in total, without registering with the Ministry of Public Information. The complainants argued that the RPA facility requirement is too stringent and has the effect of a licensure, which is prohibited by the Constitution; and motioned for constitutional review of the statute. The court granted the motion, referring the case to the Court on January 19, 1990.

---

13) Ibid., 145ff.

B. Issue of the case

RPA requiring periodical publishers to maintain and safeguard a certain level of facilities did not violate the Constitution? : Legally requiring periodical publishers to maintain and safeguard a certain level of facilities for sound growth of the press must clearly be distinguished from interfering with the essential contents of freedom of speech and press. Registration is not required for formulating and presenting views, nor for gathering and diseminating information - the substantive freedom of press - but is required of the business entity and the facilities that are the means of reporting and periodicals publication. They can be required to be registered without infringing the essential content of freedom of speech and press.

Article 7 (1) cannot profess to be an abuse of the legislative discretion violating the rule against excessive restriction or arbitrary legislation.

C. Personal opinion (Lee, Su-rim)

I have the same view precedent. That the facility needs to register a regular press material, the nature of freedom of the press and I think that this is not the infringement.

However, "the facility" should be interpreted as self-ownership with the money to discriminate against him, as no man is contrary to the principle of equality.

Will not be practical for the registration of a licensing system to ease the requirements. Additionally, humans basic rights freedom of speech and press to ensure, but up to the task periodicals publishers must be responsible.

Prohibition of labor dispute by public sector laborers case[14]
(노동쟁의조정법에 관한 헌법소원)
88Hun-Ma5, March 11, 1993

A. Summary of the case

This case was filed a consitutional complainant by an employee who work in ministry of postal communication, who is also a member of the national postal workers union and the chairman of the national federation of civil servants unions. This person insisted that Article 12 (2) of the Labor Dispute Adjustment Act infringed the fight to collective action which was enacted in Article 33 (2) of the Constitution.

B. Issue of the law

What the issue of this case is whether Article 12 (2) of the Labor Dispute Adjustment Act is nonconforming to Article 33 (2) of the Constitution or not.

The court found Article 12 (2) of the Act nonconforming to the constitution.

14) Ibid., 252ff.

1) reason 1 : Article 33 (2) of the Constitution does not entirely ban right to collective action to public employees and permits certain employees such right to collective action as including right to organization and collective bargaining. The constitution delegates to statutes the task of determining the scope of the permissible employees.

2) reason 2 : Article 12 (2) of the Act facially denies the right to collective action, in other words right to engage in dispute, to all public employees. It denies the right even to those public employees who should have been granted that right under Article 33 (2) of the Constitution. Therefore it violates the rule against excessive restriction and the essence of the basic rights themselves.

Even though the court found that the Act wasn't in accord with the Constitution, they eliminate the defect by the end of 1995, after which the provision shall be void of not revised, because they demand the legislature to realize the constitutional mandate in form of a law.

Opposite Opinion : By justice Byun Jeong-soo - he said that the provision infringes upon the essence of the three labor rights, and that the court has no legal ground to withhold immediate invalidation and merely issue a demand to the National Assembly.

C. Personal opinion (Kim, Kun-young)

In my opinion, it is true that the Act is in conflict with the Constitution. So the fact can not justify even in Article 37 (2) of the Constitution. But the Constitution connote that some public employees can have the right to collective action so it also has constitutionality, I think. Therefore the provision just need to be revised and amended for constitutionality. That is, I agree to the views of the majority in the court. And I hope this kinds of revisions will be o reate in short period, as soos as possible it can. That is legislature's duty and also for people in Korea.

CASE 15

Billiard Hall Entry Restriction case[15)]
(체육시설의 설치이용에 관한 법률 시행규칙 제5조에 대한 헌법소원)
92Hun-Ma80, May 13, 1993

A. Summary of the case

In this case, Article 5 of the Rules enforcing the Installation and Utilization of Sports Facilities Act that required billiard halls to post certain signs was struck down. This provision regulates the facility, equipment, etc and requires billiard halls "to post a notice on the door of the entrance prohibiting persons under eighteen from entering." The complainant had recently opened Billiard Hall and filed a constitutional complaint arguing that the above provision infringes upon his freedom to choose occupation

B. Issue of the law

1) freedom to choose occupation : Article 5 of the Rules which imposes duty to notice prohibiting persons under eighteen from entering eliminates a certain range of customers from the complainant's clientele.

---

15) Ibid., 202ff.

Therefore, it does limit all billiard hall operators in their freedom to pursue their occupations guaranteed by the Constitution.

2) right of equality of the Constitution : This problematic Act and its Rule subject only billiard halls to the duty to post a notice and limit their clientele. It is difficult to be seen as reasonable discrimination in comparison to other sports facilities. Article 5 of the Rules discriminates only against billiard hall operators amongst all other operators of sports facilities, and violates the Article 11(1) right of equality of the Constitution.

3) delegation of parental statute : Such restriction or ban on entry into billiard halls should be done by a statute or a regulation authorized by a statutory mandate that specifies the concrete scope of the regulation. This provision regulates matters not delegated to it by its parental statute, and deviates from the scope of delegation.

C. Personal opinion (Park, Jin-a)

I agree with the opinion of Constitutional Court. Some people might say that we should consider the importance of educational point of view because the access to the billiard hall could bring the negative effects especially for juvenile. However, the problems among the youths are not totally related to the sports facilities that they can access, but to the overall social circumstances around them and how they act toward it. Furthermore, Discrimination against only to the billiard hall operators is not make sense at all.

CASE 16

Redress for illegally-fired Civil Servants case[16)]

(1980년해직공무원의보상등에관한특별조치법 제2조 제1항 및
제5조에 대한 헌법소원)

90Hun-Ba22, etc., May 13, 1993

A. Summary of the case

The complainants, the former employees of the state-controlled entities, who were terminated in the purification plan of the National Security Emergency Measures Council in July 1980, sought compensation from their employers or successor corporation for reason of Article 2 and 5 of the Act on Special Measures, and at the same time requested constitutional review of that statue. When denied, they filed a constitutional complaint at the court.

B. Issue of the law

What the issue of this case is whether Article 2 and 5 of the Act on Special Measures concerning compensation is nonconforming to Article 11 of the Constitution or not.

The statue was not struck down for lack of the required six votes.

16) Ibid., 254ff.

Even though five justices joined in an opinion of unconstitutionality on grounds that Article 2 and 5 of the Special Compensation Act violates the principle of equality, four joined to dismiss the complaint for not meeting the legal prerequisites such as whether its resolution forms the premise of the underlying proceeding.

An opinion of unconstitutionality of the Act : ① The presiding court cannot dismiss the underlying suit in event of the Court's decision of unconstitutionality. So, this complaint does form the premise of the underlying suit. ② The legislative purpose of the statute is to provide compensation and restoration of honor to the victims of illegal and unjust exercises of governmental power by the National Security Emergency Measure Council on the basis of whether they are employees of the state or the state controlled entities. Thereforelled ecompensation plan that distinguishes the victims of the same exercise of governmental power violates Article 11(1) of the Constitution, the principle of equality.

An opinion of dismiss of the Act : ① Article 2 and 4 provides compensation or special reinstatement in limited circumstances only to public employees. ② Article 5 concerns state controlled entities but only amounts to a declaration that the state should provide 'administrative guidance' to them so that they provides their employees with the same benefits as public employees. Also administrative guidance is not legally binding and only requests voluntary cooperation of the other party. Therefore Article 5 does not apply to the underlying suit and obviously, its constitutionality does not form its premise.

C. Personal opinion (Kim, Kun-young)

I have same opinion with the 4 justices who argued to dismiss the case. Officially, the statue is titled the Special Compensation Act for

Public employees. Besides, as I have mentioned above, administrative guidance does not have binding power legally and at the same time, it amounts de facto to recommendation. So it is right that the suit was dismissed.

Kukje Group Dissolution case[17)
(공권력행사로 인한 재산권 침해에 관한 헌법소원)
89Hun-Ma31, July 29, 1993

A. Summary of the case

In this case, the Constitutional Court held that those exercises of governmental power aimed at dissolution of Kukje Group, as de facto exercise of power, violated equality and freedom of entrepreneurship, and therefore were unconstitutional.

Kukje group dissolved by Korea First Bank which receive President's direction. This situation kept a strict secrete. President instructed Korea First Bnak to prepare for the dissolution by taking control of the finance of the Group's member companies and obtaining the right to dispose of them.

The complainant filed a constitutional complaint, demanding nullification of the following series of exercises of governmental power for infringing of his basic rights.

---

17) Ibid., 205ff.

B. Issue of the law

1) Legal basis of event of government power through Minister of Finance by President's indication. : President does not notified fair notice. And exercise of the presidential authority is subject to the requirements of due process set up within the boundaries of the Constitution and the mandate of government by the rule of law. But president didn't. The legal basis does not exist.

2) Violated of right : Exercise of power, violated equality and freedom of entrepreneurship and therefore were unconstitutional. Such intervention does not show respect for economic freedom and creative of enterprises in Article 118 (1) of the Constitution. This situation property rights infringement by event of clear government power.

3) Aftermath of case : The decision clearly declared the meaning of the rule of law and established the meaning of equality and market economy.

C. Personal opinion (Lee, Soo-jeen)

President active is baseless statutory. So decision of Kukje Group Dissolution is unconstitutional. No matter what how well intended restrictions on individual's rights and imposition of responsibility must be predictable statues. Exercise of governmental power without any statutory basic violate the procedural requirements of the rule of law.

Repurchase Period Limitation case[18)]
(공공용지의취득및손실보상에관한특례법 제9조 제1항 위헌제청)
92Hun-Ka15, etc., February 24, 1994

A. Summary of the case

In this case, the Constitutional Court upheld Article 9 (1) of the Act on Special Cases concerning the Acquisition of Lands for Public Use and the Compensation for Their Loss that limits the period in which the seller could repurchase the land.

The claimants requested constitutional review of the said provision which requires that the purchased lands become unneeded 'within ten years of the acquisition,' in order for the original sellers to gain the right to repurchase, citing violation of right to property. The Changwon District Court granted the motion and referred the case to the Constitutional Court for review.

B. Issue of the law

1) target of judgment : In the case of the referee's target of the

---

18) Ibid., 208ff.

abolition of public enterprises such changes due to other reasons, such as land acquisition will require all or part of the limit on the maximum period when the "within ten years of the acquisition," part of Whether that is in violation of the Constitution.

2) whether that is in violation of the Constitution? : The limit on the maximum period in which such right to repurchase could be granted is needed, and the period of "ten years from the date of acquisition" in Article 9 (1) of the Act is not so short as to lose appropriateness. Therefore, it does not conflict with the basic constitutional ideas concerning the guarantee of people's right to property.

3) legislative discretion problem : (Another opinion) Is the contents and conditions of the right to repurchase should be, in principle, left to the legislative discretion and does not implicate the right to property. Article 9 (1) of the Act does not violate the Constitution.

C. Personal opinion (Lee, Su-rim)

I agree major opinion. The right to recover the ownership of the land unneeded or unused for the public project pursuant to Article 71 of the Land Expropriation Act is derived from, and therefore included in, the constitutional guarantee of right to property. The right to repurchase in Article 9 of the Act should be treated equally as the right to repurchase in Article 71 of the Land Expropriation Act and included in the content of property right protected by the Constitution.

The limit on the maximum period of right to repurchase, I think, this is not the infringement of the nature property right.

National Seat Succession case[19]
(전국구국회의원 의석계승 미결정 위헌확인)
92Hun-Ma153, April 28, 1994

A. Summary of the case

Reunification National Party earned seven national seats in the 14th National Assembly election conducted on March 24th, 1992. On June 11th of that year, Cho Yun-hyoung, a member from national seats, left the party. The Party requested the Commission to transfer his seat to a successor within the Party. The Commission refused, citing lack of provisions in the old Election of National Assembly Members Act. The Party brought a constitutional complaint before the Court questioning the constitutionality of the Commission's forbearance.

B. Issue of the law

1) Whether or not a member from national seats defecting from his party leaves his seat vacant.

it depends on the legal relationship between the assembly persons who

19) Ibid., 174ff.

are people's representatives and the people who elect them. Article 7 (1) of the Constitution states, "public officials shall be servants of the entire people and shall be responsible to the people." Article 45 also states, "no member of the National Assembly shall be held responsible outside the National Assembly for the opinions officially expressed, or the votes cast, in the Assembly." Article 46 (2) states, "members of the National Assembly shall give the first priority to national interests and shall perform their duties in accordance with their conscience." All these provisions, taken together, put assemblypersons on their own discretion pursuant to the principle of free mandate and, therefore, their membership is not affected by their defection from a party that nominated them to their seats.

2) The constitutionality of the Commission's forbearance.

Even if there is a vacancy, the National Election Commission have not received a notice of vacancy from the Speaker of the House; therefore, the Commission has no duty to transfer the vacant seat to a successor. The complaint does not meet the legal prerequisites.

3) Legislative solution.

During the review, the problem found a legislative solution when a provision was inserted into Article 192 (4) of the Act on the Election of Public Officials and the Prevention of Election Malpractices to the effect that a member from national seats loses his seat when he defects or changes his party or affiliates with two parties, except in case of merger or dissolution of his party or his expulsion from the party.

C. Personal opinion (Cheong, Han-sae-beol)

A member from national seat elected through party vote is more likely to be bound by party affiliation compared to a member from regional one. The succession of party membership means loss of the relation of confidence and mandate. Also the so-called "migratory bird politicians" change the party, ignoring the opinion of the people. Such attitude should be regulated on real politik. However, Article 192 (4) of the Act on the Election of Public Officials and the Prevention of Election Malpractices is contrast to the principle of free mandate because the provision enables party affiliation to be legally bound and is available to violate Article 8 (2) of the Constitution providing introparty democracy. Moreover, this provision violates the principle of equality and infringes upon the privilege of equality and the right to hold public office, by distinguishing the member from national seat from the member from regional one.

Land Excess-Profits Tax Act case[20]
(토지초과이득세법 제10조 등 위헌소원)
92Hun-Ba49, etc., July 29, 1994

A. Summary of the case

The complainants filed for judicial review of administrative action at the Seoul High Court, demanding nullification of the tax when the tax office director categorized their lands under the above said Article 8(1) (iv) and 8(1)(ⅹⅲ) and imposed the land excess-profits tax. They also requested constitutional review of Article 8, 11 and 12 of the statute on grounds that those provisions violated the principle of statutory taxation in Articles 38 and 59 of the Constitution and its Article 119 describing our economic order. When denied at the High Court, they filed a constitutional complaint.

B. Issue of the law

Constitutional review of Land Excess-Profits Tax Act, Article 8, 11, 12. 1) Article 8(1)(iv) : Taxation overly focuses on efficient use of the

---

20) Ibid., 211ff.

land and gives incentives for unplanned and disorderly constructions designed solely to make immediate use of the land. It does not harmonize well with the latter statute in a legislative scheme and contradicts the constitutional right to humane livelihood and the constitutional duties of the State to guarantee social welfare and comfortable residential life.

2) Article 8(1)(x iii) : Existence of the tax obligation is determined by administrative authority without any legislative control. This is a conflict with the principle of statutory taxation in Article 59 of the Constitution. The provision also discriminates against the lessors more than it does other owners solely because they are not using the lands themselves. This is a conflict with Article 119 of the Constitution.

3) Article 11 : Standard public land prices have so great a consequence on the existence and the scope of people's tax obligations that their determination is not adequate for blanket delegation to lower laws. They should be outlined at least generally in the statutory provisions. Thereby violating the principle of statutory taxation in Articles 38 and 59 of the Constitution and the Article 75 requirement that the scope of delegation be specific.

4) Article 12 : When applied to the unrealized gains that are by nature difficult to be measured objectively, is so high that it may constitute tax on artificial gains and again engulf the principal, violating right to property. Subjecting it to a uniform rate impedes substantive equality among taxpayers at different income levels.

5) Article 26(1), (4) : Allows only a portion of the land excess-profits tax to be deducted from the transfer profit tax when the former is by nature a prepayment of the latter since they completely overlap in the objects of taxation and have similar purposes. Failure to allow deduction of the entire amount of the excess land value tax from the transfer profit tax violates the principle of taxation on real worth, a component of the constitutional principle of taxation by law.

C. Personal opinion (Park, Hye-ju)

I agree with Constitutional Court decision.

The Act needs to be amended since some parts of the Act violate the Constitution while others do not conform to the Constitution. Nevertheless, the above statute is intricately related in content and structure to other tax laws like the Restitution of Development Gains Act. Its invalidation will create confusion and vacuum in law both in the legislative and financial sectors. The Court hereby gives a decision of nonconformity to the Constitution whereby the Act remains in effect formally until it is abolished or amended by the legislators pursuant to the above mentioned reasons of unconstitutionality. However, it is not to be applied to or enforced in any future case by the ordinary courts and other state agencies in the meantime.

CASE 21

Local Government Election Postponement Case[21]

(지방자치단체의 장 선거일 불공고 위헌 확인)

92Hun—Ma126, August 31, 1994

A. Summary of the case

This case would have questioned unconstitutionality of the presidential measures postponing the first local government heads election ever in our history: but was dismissed because a statue was enacted during the review to justify the postponement, eliminating the justiciable interests.

The National Assembly revised the Local Autonomy Act. The Local Autonomy Act set the date of the first election of local government heads as December 30, 1991 and later revised again to change the date to December 30, 1992 or earlier. But, Election date does not announced before presidential election 18day.

Therefore, right to vote and right to be elected are protected by constitution. Petitioner is violated right to vote and right to bo elected.

---

21) Ibid., 158ff.

B. Issue of the law

Constitutional Court all petition dismissed. The petition have a place infringement of fundamental right. However, I hard to see that is disrespect local government heads election day and basis right infringement. It is right that can exercise after pollbook creation or candidate registration.

Therefore, It is no applicant's qualification. This is job of the Administration. In this case, the Local Autonomy Act revised, so delegated legislation. Right to vote and right to be elected was protected by law.

Local Autonomy Act also revised by the National Assembly. In this case, advanced announcement are abolished and election dates are statutorily fixed : therefore, there is neither repeatability of no-announcements nor importance of constitutional clarification, Hence no justiciable interest.

C. Personal opinion (Lee, Soo-jeen)

I think that local government heads election does not composed of fundamental right. So petitioner eliminating the justiciable interests. Because local government heads election is the Administration jurisdiction. Constitutional Court is not involved in case.

CASE 22

December 12 Incident Non-institution of Prosecution case[22]
(불기소처분 취소)
94Hun-Ma246, January 20, 1995

A. Summary of the case

In this case, the Court dismissed in part and rejected in part a constitutional complaint challenging the Public Prosecutor's Office's decision not to prosecute Chun Doo-hwan, Roh Tae-woo, other members of the military junta for their involvement in the December 12 Incident. After the assassination of President Park Cheong-hi by Kim Chae-kyu, then the director of the Korean Central Intelligence Agency, left a vacuum in the executive power on October 26, 1979, the new military power arrested Martial Law Commander-in-chief Chung Sung-hwa and other military leaders, took control of the military, and practically took over the control of the state.

B. Issue of the law

1) Judge constitutional petition if whether stopped of the statute of limitations. : Constitutional petition judge sending even if group 2 of

22) Ibid., 161ff.

Article 262 of the Criminal Procedure Law to apply to the inference that suspicion fact will stop the statute of limitations can not see.

2) In the case of treason and mutiny, during the president's office for a crime whether or not the statute of limitations suspended? : Constitution and Criminal Procedure Law, etc law during the president's office will be suspended of the statute limitation does noes not clearly defined, prosecution of the country conform reason for the obstacle of the law, during the office of the president course of the statute of limitations will be suspended.

3) 12, 12 for the prosecution of the case suspension of indictment disposal beyond the scope of the discretion whether or not?

• If the conflict extenuating suspension of a sentence case, they choose any reason in principle, whether it's discretion is in the range.

• Prosecution reason is important, but 'Circumstances after the crime', Crime after the change of the social situation, over time and including changes in the inflict punishment assessment that must be construed.

C. Personal opinion (Lee, Su-rim)

According to Article 84 The President shall not be charged with a criminal offense during his tenure of office except for insurrection or treason, for the during tenure the president, he will stop the statute of limitations for the crime.

On the charge of treason · mutiny except for the crime of crimes subject to the privilege of non-prosecution it does not stop the statute of limitations, Chun Doo-hwan, Roh Tae-woo, other memberot ommit for the regime usurpation for crimes I think that this is rebellion. Therefor must be punished, and this at any time, regardless of the statute of limitations and can be punishable.

So I am opposed to the precedent of the majority opinion.

Violation of the Remedial order of the Labor Relations Commissions case[23)]
(노동조합법 제46조 위헌제청)
92Hun-Ka14, March 23, 1995

A. Summary of the case

The claimant received an order of relief from Labor Relations Commissions but it was annulled on appeal. Despite of this result, he was prosecuted summarily on charges of violating the Labor Standards Act and Labor Union Act and fined by the Cheju District Court on a summary trial. So he appealed to a full trial and requested constitutional review.

B. Issue of the law

What the issue of this case is whether the part of Article 46 that says "when the order of relief pursuant to Article 42 is violated" is nonconforming to the constitution or not.

The constitutional court struck down the part of Article 46 and the court found violations of due process of law and the rule against

---

23) Ibid., 256ff.

excessive restriction after examining the nature of remedial order.

There are two reasons ; 1) Criminal punishment for violation of an administrative order does not happen before the order is validated in court. 2) There is not legislative precedence anywhere in the world where a statutory criminal penalty if to proceed as if the order was validated when it had been annulled on appeal.

C. Personal opinion (Kim, Kun-young)

When I consider the court's opinion, I agree with the court. To punish the employer for violations of an order, the order should be finalized. That is due process of law and at the same time necessary minimum restriction of basic rights.

Standard public land price-based transfer profits tax case[24]

(소득세법 제60조에 대한 헌법소원)

91Hun-Ba1, etc., November 30, 1995

A. Summary of the case

Article 60 of the Income Tax Act delegates determination of standard public land prices, on the basis of which the tax basis for the transfer profits tax is computed, to a presidential decree. In this case, the court found the provision nonconforming to the constitution as an impermissible blanket delegation, violating the principle of statutory taxation in Article 59 of the Constitution.

The complaint filed for nullification of the transfer profits tax levied by the local Tax Office Director at an ordinary court and requested constitutional review of the former Income Tax Act, and when turned down, filed a Article 68(2) constitutional complaint.

B. Issue of the law

1) the court upheld Article 23 (4) and 45 (1) (i) of the pre-1990 Act and Article 23 (4) (i) and 45 (1) (i) (A) of the pre-1993 Act

---

24) Ibid., 219ff.

and found only Article 60 nonconforming to the Constitution.

2) The Court ordered to apply the revised provision instead of Article 60. the aforementioned Act NO. 4803 replaced Article 60 with Article 99 on Dec.22, 1994 that provided a concrete definition of a standard public land price.

3) For a land without the publicly noticed value, the standard public land price will be the amount appraised by the Tax Office Director according to the method determined by presidential decree using the publicly noticed value of similar lands in proximity. For an area with rapid price increases selected by a presidential decree, the value will be assessed using a multiplier.

4) The Court finds it nonconforming instead of issuing a simple decision of unconstitutionality. The supreme court therefore construe the Constitutional Court's decision as a proposal for applying the old Article 60 provisionally for the tax obligations incurred before the effective date of the new statute.

5) However, some might argue that the Supreme Court should have waited for the legislature to fix again the brand new statute. only if the vacuum still remains, it could exceptionally apply the old provision. Or even then, the Court could use various interpretive techniques such as analogies to solve the problem.

C. Personal opinion (Lee, Hyun-ho)

I think that adopting the standard public land prices principle (Article 60 of the pre-1994 Act) is fair and square. But, Article 60 of the pre-1994 Act which entrust the task of defining a standard public land price and the process of computing it wholly to a presidential decree without specifying any guidance or setting any limit on them is nonconf orming to the Constitution(Article 59).

Actual Transaction Price—based Transfer Profits Tax case[25)]
(소득세법 제23조 제2항 등 위헌소원)
94Hun—Ba40, etc., November 30, 1995

A. Summary of the case

In this case, the Court reviewed the provision of the Income Tax Act on transfer profits tax, which allowed the transfer value and the acquisition cost to be the actual transaction prices under the exceptional circumstances prescribed by a presidential decree. The Court found that it could be a blanket delegation violating the principle of statutory taxation and the rule against blanket delegation under limited circumstances.

B. Issue of the law

1) Whether or not the provision of computation was unconstitutional, as applying the standard of assessment.

Viewed in light of the overall structure and related provisions of the Income Tax Act, the income from transfer of realty will be considered a business income if the transfer is deemed for profit by social custom and

---

25) Ibid., 222ff.

CASE 25 • 71

amounts to a business activity in its size, frequency, and features. The incomes from these frequent and repetitive transfers are taxed together under the general income tax, and all other transfer incomes clearly fall and will be taxed under the transfer profit tax. Therefore, Article 23 (2) of the former Income Tax Act does not lack the requisite clarity as a provision defining the tax basis for the transfer profits tax.

2) The main issue is whether the provisos of Article 23 (4) and 45 (1) (i) of the former Income Tax Act which permit the use of the actual transaction prices was opposed to statutory taxation and the rule against blanket delegation.

Even though the provisos do not explicitly and directly stipulate the scope of delegation, they can be reasonably interpreted as doing so in view of the overall structure of the Income Tax Act, the nature of transfer profit tax, and the constitutional limits inherent in the standard public land price-based system.

Thus interpreted, the provisos are measures to protect taxpayers from being at a disadvantage by use of the standard public land prices, as opposed to that of the actual transaction prices. Therefore, the provisos delegate the authority of deciding when to use actual transaction prices to presidential decrees only for the situations where the tax amount thus calculated does not exceed the tax amount calculated with standard public land prices.

Thus interpreted, the provisos concretely specify the scope of delegation and do not violate the constitutional principles of statutory taxation or the rule against blanket delegation.

Whereas, if the provisos read to have departed from that scope of delegation and included in that delegation the authority for a situation where actual transaction prices produce higher tax amounts than standard public land prices, they violate the principle of statutory taxation of Articles 38 and 59 and the rule against blanket delegation of Article 75 of the Constitution to that limited extent.

C. Personal opinion (Cheong, Han-sae-beol)

I assume that the decision of the Court was constitutionally adequate. Tax regulations must be stipulated clearly without ambiguity. But even if the provision lacks the requisite clarity, Permitting the use of the actual transaction prices is reasonable according to the overall structure and related provisions of the Income Tax Act. Also I agree to the opinion that the provisos of Article 23 (4) and 45 violates the Constitution insofar as they are interpreted as allowing the presidential decree to use the actual transaction prices when it results in a higher tax amount than the standard public land price.

CASE 26

May 18 Incident Non-institution of Prosecution Decision case[26)
(불기소처분취소)
95Hun-Ma221, etc., December 15, 1995

A. Summary of the case

In this case, the Court reviewed a constitutional complaint against the prosecutor's decision not to prosecute the violent suppression of the Kwangju Democratization Movement on May 18, 1980. This case arose out of three different criminal complaints against the main actors of the May 18 Incident.

1) The first one was filed by the victims of the violent suppression, charging treason, murder with treasonous intent, and mutiny against Chun Doohwan and twenty four other major figures in the military junta (95Hun-Ma221, filed on May 13, 1994).

2) The second one was filed by Kim Dae-jung and others victimized by the fabricated charges of treasonous conspiracy, charging treason, attempted murder with treasonous intent, and munity against Chun Doo-hwan and ten others (95Hun-Ma233, filed on October 19, 1994).

3) The third one was filed by others, charging treason and mutiny against Chun Doo-hwan and thirty five others (95Hun-Ma297).

---

26) Ibid., 164ff.

B. Issue of the law

The Constitutional Court declared the case closed upon the complainants' withdrawal pursuant to Article 40 of the Constitutional Court Act interpreted in light of Article 239 of the Civil Procedure Act, forming the Court's opinion.

Justices posited that the Court could proceed to a final ruling even if the complainants had withdrawn.

1) Emphasized the objective function of the constitutional complaint process and opined that the Court should publish the opinion as the Justices have previously agreed.

2) Reasoned that, if the complainants withdraw, the case should be closed with respect to its subjective portion, namely giving relief to claims of rights. But, the objective function of the constitutional complaint process demands that it should continue on to a final decision with respect to those issues resolution of which are vital to defense of the constitutional order, if there are such issues.

In this case, the question of punishability of a successful coup calls for a constitutional answer because it affects the fate of this nation and the basic rights of all people, and demands a final decision irrespective of the complainants' withdrawal. Before the withdrawal, a super-majority of the justices had agreed that a successful coup is punishable during the deliberation. The new majority that declared the case closed acquiesced with the minority's publication of a part of the previously agreed-upon final decision irrespective of the complaints' withdrawal.

C. Personal opinion (Park, Hye-ju)

A successful treason becomes not punishable under the exceptional circumstances that the people have ratified it through free expressions of their sovereign wills.

In this case, the treasonous acts of the two former Presidents were neither justified by the circumstances nor were ratified by free expressions of the people (Denying legitimacy of the treasonous government does not mean denying the legal effects of all of its acts). The prosecutor's non-institution of prosecution decision for reason of immunity of a successful coup engenders misunderstanding of the ideals of the Constitution and the criminal jurisprudence of treason.

Excessive Electoral District
Population Disparity case[27]
(공직선거및선거부정방지법의 국회의원 지역선거구
구역표 위헌확인)
95Hun-Ma224, etc., December 27, 1995

A. Summary of the case

The smallest district is the 'Chonnam Changheung County' district with a population of 61,529. And districts of complainants are 3times larger. overall, about one fifth of the 260 electoral districts in total showed a population disparity larger than 3:1 with the smallest district. In addition, the new 'Chung-Buk Boeun & Youngdong Counties' district was originally linked to the district of Okchun County, the three counties forming one electoral district. The new Table turned the Okchun County into a separate district, leaving the new district composed of the Boeun and Youngdong Counties which are geographically separated.

B. Issue of the law

1) The principle of equal election and equal weight of votes.
• one man, one vote and one vote, one value.

---

27) Ibid., 176ff.

It not only refutes multiple votes, carries a meaning of equality in the number of votes, and recognizes one person one vote for all, but also mandates equality in their weight, that is, the extent that one vote contributes to the entire system of election.

2) The permissible limit of population disparity.

• Justices deffered on the permissible limit of population disparity.

• The common opinion : set the permissible maximum ratio between the most populous district and the least at 4:1, or equivalently set the permissible maximum deviation from the average district at 60%.

3) Issue of the gerrymandering.

• In this case, without any extraordinary reason of inevitability, the Boeun County and the Youngdong County that are completely separated from each other by the Okchun County in the middle are joined in one electoral district. Such redistricting is arbitrary and departs from the scope of legislative discretion.

4) Decision

• the national assembly election redistricting plan is unconstitutional.

• The requisition of complainant is rejects.

C. Personal opinion (Kim, Eun-ho)

I don't agree to this rejection. I agree to Justices Cho Seung-hyung and Kim Chin-woo. Indivisibility recognize from this decision. But this decision is inconsistency from article 1 and 2 of the text. So, my opinion is Only the 'Haewoondae & Kijang County' and 'Boeun & Youngdong County' is unconstitutional. And will not be able to reject.

Mandatory Filing Stamp case[28]
(민사소송 등 인지법 제1조 등 위헌소원)
93Hun-Ba57, August 29, 1996

A. Summary of the case

The complainant filed a suit against the state for emotional damages for a governmental tort, but was ordered by the court to affix stamps to the complaint. Upon such order, the complainant claimed economic hardship and requested aid for litigation costs, but was turned down for not having made a showing that he will not clearly lose on merits. Consequently, the complainant requested constitutional review of the provision requiring the stamps even on complaints against the state, alleging infringement upon right to trial, and when denied, filed a constitutional complaint.

B. Issue of the law

1) Rejects a requisition about article 2 of the Act on the Costs for civil Litigation.

---

28) Ibid., 225ff.

2) The Constitutional Court upheld Article 1 of the Act on the Stamps Attached for civil Litigation.

• This decision is unanimous.

Article 1 of the Act on the Stamps Attached for Civil Litigation, etc. requires a certain amount of stamps to be affixed to all complaints. Insofar as the current civil procedure is equipped with a system of providing aids for litigation costs, such requirement does not hamper or obstruct completely the indigent's opportunity for a trial, nor infringe upon right to trial nor discriminate irrationally.

Furthermore, the present Act on the Stamps Attached for Civil Litigation, etc. unified the rates for all civil suits to 5/1000 (Article 2(1)) of the amounts in controversy, which is the lowest so far and therefore has reduced the burden on the people. Objectively, the rate is not so high as to infringe upon right to trial or the constitutional principle of equality,

C. Personal opinion (Kim, Eun-ho)

I agree to this decision. As the current civil procedure is equipped with a system of providing aids for litigation costs, such requirement does not hamper or obstruct completely the indigent's opportunity for a trial, nor infringe upon right to trial nor discriminate irrationally.

Motion Pictures Pre-Inspection case[29)]
(영화법 제12조 등 위헌제청)
93Hun-Ka13, etc., October 4, 1996

A. Summary of the case

The combined cases, 93Hun-Ka13 and 91Hun-Ba10, arose out of motions for constitutional review by the claimants who were brought to the Seoul District Criminal Court for violating the Motion Picture Act(hereafter MPA) by showing 'Opening the Closed Gate to the School' in 1992 and 'Oh, Country of Dream' in 1989 respectively without pre-inspection of the ethics committee.

The first claimant made the motion when prosecuted, and the court accepted, referring the case to the Court for review.

The second, already convicted and imposed a one million won fine, made the motion in appeal of that conviction, but was denied.

B. Issue of the law

1) Constitutional protection about motion picture production and

---

29) Ibid., 150ff.

showing.

2) Meaning the principle of prohibition of censorship under the Article 21 (2) of the constitution.

3) Constitutional or unconstitutional about part of the consideration by the public performance ethics committee in Article 12 (1) and (2) and Article 13 (1) of the MPA.

4) Decision

• A motion picture is a form of expression, and its production and showing should be protected by the Article 21 (1) freedom of speech and press. It is protected also under the Article 22 (1) freedom of Science and arts since often used as means to publish the results of academic research of as a form of art.

• Omission.

• Deliberation About motion picture in Article 12 (1) and (2) and Article 13 (1) of the MPA is pre-inspection forbidden by the constitution. Also the Public Performance Ethics Committee is a censorship body. Because of continuous affect on administrative body about form of the Public Performance Ethics Committee.

C. Personal opinion (Kim, Eun-ho)

Article 21 of constitution guarantees freedom of speech and press. And Article 22 of constitution guarantees freedom of science and arts. Motion picture is means of declaration of intention, artistic expression and publication of investigation. So motion picture production and showing are guaranteed with constitution.

Local Soju Compulsory Purchase System case[30] (주세법 제38조의 7 등에 대한 위헌제청) 96Hun-ka18, December 26, 1996

A. Summary of the case

Article 38-7(1) of the Liquor Tax Act provided that soju wholesalers must purchase more than 50% of the total monthly purchase from the producers located in the same province or city. If the above provision was violated, director of the tax office was allowed to suspend the liquor sales or the license. The claimant was suspended from operating his business by the local tax office for violation of problematic provision. After that, the claimant sought nullification of the administrative action and requested constitutional review of the provision at the same time.

B. Issue of the law

1) soju wholesalers' occupational freedom : The Liquor Tax Act seeks to maintain one soju maker in every province and it largely limits wholesalers' right to decide certain company what they want, whether to

30) Ibid., 228ff.

purchase or not, and proper quantity. In addition, there is no relation between promoting regional economy and maintaining one soju maker in each province.

2) soju makers' freedom of competition and entrepreneurship : To protect the small-to-midsize businesses as a national economic policy goal, it must be realized by strengthening the rules of competition. The compulsory purchase system cannot be an appropriate means to achieve public interest.

3) consumers' right to self-determination

4) the right of equality : In relation to equality, if the compulsory local purchase were aimed at monopoly regulation and protection of small-to-midsize enterprises, there is no rational reason to apply it only to soju wholesalers among all other wholesalers.

C. Personal opinion (Park, Jin-a)

I agree with the decision of constitutional court. To restrain monopoly by a big business and protect regional economy, there could be various ways to achieve this goal by such as helping minor companies financially at second hand to develop manufacturing system or R&D program. Especially the 50% regional market share is not only harsh for wholesalers but also solidifies the regional monopoly which is potentially against the national economic policy goal to protect regional economic development.

Livelihood Protection Standard case[31]

(1994년 생계보호기준 위헌확인)

94Hun–Ma33, May 29, 1997

A. Summary of the case

The complainants, husband and wife, were protected under Article 6(1) of the Protection of Minimum Living Standards Act and Article 6 (i) of the regulation, and were recipients of the living assistance payment calculated under "the 1994 Livelihood Protection Standard" in the 1994 Guidelines for Livelihood Protection Programs, which was promulgated by the Minister of Health and Welfare in January. the couple filed a constitutional complaint against the "1994 Livelihood Protection Standard", that the amount of the payment was far led than the minimum living cost and therefore infringed on the constitutionally guaranteed right to pursuit of happiness and humane livelihood.

B. Issue of the law

1) The Constitutional Court dismissed the case, holding that the

---

31) Ibid., 239ff.

"1994 Livelihood Protection Standard" does not violate the Constitution.

2) Constitutionality of the livelihood protection standards set bathe administration cannot be judged on the living assistance payment under the Protection of Minimum Living Standards Act alone but on the aggregate including those living protection payments or exemptions provided by other laws.

3) In consideration of all these benefits, even if their aggregate sum does not meet that year's minimum cost of living for a household of two that fact alone does not render the "1994 Livelihood Protection Standard" state's failure in providing for the objective minimum necessary for humane livelihood or a clear departure from the constitutionally permitted scope of discretion.

4) It did not violate the complainants' right to pursue happiness and to humane livelihood or otherwise violate the Constitution.

5) Critics of the decision, however, argued that the Court was excessively conscious of the impact that the state's active intervention in the sphere of public benefits would bring about on its fiscal uneconomic policies and allowed too broad a policy discretion to the state in its setting of the level of protection for the people without economic ability.

C. Personal opinion (Lee, Hyun-ho)

I think that it could be violated to the Constitution as far as if the state be an situation that an object of judicial judgment that to be an life worthy of humane being, the state entirely does not legislation about livelihood protection or the contents is so irrational about the contents that sphere of discretion which is admitted to constitution is clearly deviate remarkably. So, I agree the judicial decision.

Legislative Railroading case[32)

(국회의원과 국회의장간의 권한쟁의)

96Hun–Ra2, July 16, 1997

A. Summary of the case

In the 182nd session of the National Assembly on Dec 23, 1996, the opposition party members opposing the immature passage of the bills interfered with the proceeding. Then the vice-Speaker, on behalf of the Speaker, convened session by notifying only the members of the ruling party and declared the passage of the bills by those present. On the 30th of the month, the members of opposition petitioned for review of the competence dispute. Constitutional Court held that the speaker's railroading of a bill violated the rights to review and vote on proposed legislation; however, Court held that it does not a clear violation of the provisions of the Constitution.

B. Issue of the law

1) justiciability requirements(whether the individual member of NA

---

32) Ibid., 179ff.

can be the parties): Article 62(1)(i) of the constitution was no a definitive or enumerative provision but rather an illustrative one. Therefore the individual representatives and the Speaker are state agencies and can be parties to competence disputes.

2) the right to review and vote: The opposition party members cannot be expected to be present at the meeting on such a late notification or lack of notification and it does not clearly meet the requirements of Article 76(3) of the National Assembly Act. Since the respondent Speaker's violation of this Article extinguished the plaintiffs' opportunity to attend the meeting and to review and vote on proposed bills, such act clearly violated the plaintiffs' power granted by the Constitution.

3) unconstitutionality of the passage of bills:

3justices(−) Bills mentioned in this case were passed by the majority of the representatives which was not closed to the media or ordinary citizens in any way. Therefore, although violation of the National Assembly Act might be a blemish, there was no clear violation of the principle of majority vote and the principle of open session by the Constitution.

3justices(+) Majority vote should be based on the opportunity to attend provided to all the members who could be notified of the meeting and this act infringed on the plaintiffs' powers to review and vote and violates Article 49.

C. Personal opinion (Park, Jin−a)

Notification only to the certain party and thus passage of bills completely violates the procedures-majority vote-specified by the Constitution. The principle of due process of law applies to legislative procedures as well. How could the Constitutional Court ignore this point even after they noticed the right to review and vote the Speaker infringed on.

Same–Surname–Same–Origin Marriage Ban case[33)]

(민법 제809조 제1항 위헌제청)

95Hun–Ka6, etc., July 16, 1997

A. Summary of the Case

The Court held that Article 809 (1) of the Civil Code was incompatible with the Constitution, and that if the National Assembly did not amend it by December 31, 1998, it would become null and void, starting on January 1, 1999. Until the National Assembly amended the Marriage Prohibition Clause, other courts and government agencies, including local governments, should not apply the Clause.

Article 809 (1) of the Civil Act prohibits marriage between two persons who have the same family name and come from the same ancestral line("Dongsungdongbon").

The ban on same-surname-same-origin marriage has been the subject of a long dispute between the Confucian adherents who emphasize its unity with the national tradition and the women's groups who demand its revision or abolition on the ground that it is not only too broad a prohibition on marriage without any genetic evidence but also a relic of patriarchy and male supremacy. As interim solutions,

---

33) Ibid., 242ff.

The National Assembly, using the Act on Special Cases concerning Marriage, saved many same-surname-same-origin couples from the hardship in schooling of their children and their marriage life by recognizing their de facto marital status. It, however, failed to provide a final resolution on the issue. Eventually, the provision came to the Constitutional Court for constitutional review.

The claimants who would like to marry people with same surnames from same ancestral lines sought nullification of the administrative action that rejected their marriage registrations in the Seoul Family Court and requested constitutional review of the provision.

The Family Court accepted the request and referred the issue to the Constitutional Court on May 17, 1995. As the case came to the Constitutional Court, the Confucian adherent groups made substantial efforts to deter the Court from striking down the provision by sending petitions to the Justices.

B. Issue of the law

The issue was whether Article 809 (1) of the Civil Code ("Marriage Prohibition Clause") which prohibits marriage between two persons of the same family name from the same origin was constitutional.

C. Personal opinion (Cheong, Han-sae-beol)

The legislative purpose of the Marriage Prohibition Clause did not fall under the permissible category of restricting individual human rights for "social order" or "public welfare" prescribed in Article 37 (2) of the Constitution. Such prohibition also violated the equal protection clause of the Constitution by discriminating against gender, because it applied only to surnames from the same patrilineal blood. Also, the Marriage Prohibition Clause infringed upon the pursuit of happiness, which includes the freedom to choose one's spouse, and was inconsistent with the right to marry guaranteed by Article 36 (1) of the Constitution. I assume the decision of the Court was adequate for such reasons.

Priority of Employees' Retirement Allowances case[34]

(근로기준법 제30조의2 제2항 위헌소원)

94Hun—Ba19, etc., August 21, 1997

A. Summary of the case

The Industrial Bank of Korea filed a lawsuit against the debtor's retiring employees objecting to distribution of assets at the Suwon District Court. But that court rejected so the claimant requested constitutional review of the statute on the portion concerning 'retirement allowances'.

B. Issue of the law

What the issue of this case is whether the 'retirement allowances' portion of Article 30-2 of the former Labor Standards Act and Article 37(2) of the Labor Standards Act is nonconforming to the constitution or not. The court found the 'retirement allowance' portion of Article 30-2 of the former Standards Act and Article 37(2) of the Labor Standards Act nonconforming to the Constitution and ordered that

---

34) Ibid., 258ff.

portion will become voed on January 1, 1998 if it is not revised by the legislature till December 31, 1997. The court ordered that, in the meantime, courts, state agencies ot lacal governments suspend its application.

1) REASON 1 : The 'retirement allowance' portion of the provision may infringe on the essential content of rights arising out of mortg ages and pledges.

2) REASON 2 : The provision is not appropriate as a means of restricting the secured creditors' right to advance the public interest of workers' welfare and also violates the mandates of minimum restriction and balancing of interests.

C. Personal opinion (Kim, Kun-young)

I also have same opinion with the court concerning this case. The part of the retirement allowance of the Act was enacted to guarantee livelihood and social security but on the other hand, this provision violates the essential right of property which is secured constitutionally and at the same time this violation of the rule against excessive restriction. So that is why I can say it is unconstitutional.

Violation of collective bargaining Agreement case[35)]
(노동조합법 제46조의3 위헌제청)
96Hun-Ka20, March 26, 1998

A. Summary of the case

A worker of an company in the Greater city of Woolsan was prosecuted on the Woolsan Branch of the Pusan District Court for violating Article 46-3 of the Labor union Act. He violated peace clause of the collective bargaining agreement by instigating fellow workers to engage in labor dispute. The presiding court requested constitutional review of the provision that it may violate the principle of statutory punishment.

B. Issue of the law

What the issue of this case is whether Article 46-3 of the former Labor Union Act that imposes a fine up to 10 million won for violation of a collective bargaining agreement is nonconforming to the constitution or not.

---

35) Ibid., 261ff.

The court struck down the Article 46-3 of the above mentioned Labor Union Act.

1) REASON 1: The provision at least have specified which item on a collective bargaining agreement upon a violation. Article 46-3 of the Act makes no such attempt and simply state 'violation of a collective bargaining agreement'. It merely describes the outer shell of the elements of a crime and leaves their essential content, the real kernel of the prohibition, to the collective bargaining process.

2) REASON 2: The provision completely fails to provide for predictability, one of the essential elements of the principle of nulla poena sine lege. Besides, the above provision, overly ambiguous and broad on its elements, violates the principle of clarity, another component of the principle of nulla poena sine lege.

C. Personal opinion (Kim, Kun-young)

As all justice have same decisions, I also have a same thought with them. It is obvious true that the law should be precise and clear and have a exact limit of application. The above mentioned act violates this point, so it is, of course, unconstitutional.

Case on Registration Revocation of Obscenity Publishers[36]
(출판사및인쇄소의등록에관한법률 제5조의2 제5호 등 위헌제청)
95Hun-Ka16, April 30, 1998

A. Summary of the case

Fact pattern : The Seocho District Office of City of Seoul revoked registration of the petitioner under the name Jongin Enterprise Publishing for publishing and distributing the so-called 'Semi-Girl' photo binder ("nine actress semi-girls nice photographs") on the grounds that it was indecent or obscene. The petitioner sought judicial review of the revocation at the Seoul High Court whereupon he made a motion for constitutional review under Article 21 (1) (freedom of press), and with Article 11 (equality) of the Constitution. The High Court referred the case to the Constitutional Court.

B. Issue of the law

1) The standard for judging whether the content of speech and press is denied the constitutional protection. (The scope of permitted expression)

36) Ibid., 154ff.

The governmental and legal regulation of the content of speech and press is more likely to interfere with the free exchange of ideas, but if the harm of the ills cannot be cured by self-cleansing mechanism of civil society, state intervention is permitted as the primary and freedom of speech and press not protected under the constitution.

2) The differentiation between indecent and obscene materials.

The standard for judging obscenity is whether the dominant theme of the material taken as a whole appeals to prurient interest in sex. Obscenity is without redeeming social importance. whereas indecency contains sexual or excretory material that does not rise to the level of obscenity.

3) Whether or not the revocation of publisher's registration for publishing obscene or indecent materials is unconstitutional.

Obscenity is hardly likely to change in meaning due to the individual flavors of the person applying the law, therefore does not violate the rule of clarity. and the impairment of the basic rights is not severe whereas the public interest and the need for banning and suppressing obscene publications is overwhelming. The provision does not violate the prohibition of excessive restriction. The concept of 'indecency' justifying revocation of registration is so broad and abstract that a judge's supplementary interpretation cannot sharpen its meaning, and therefore does not inform a publisher's decision in adjusting the contents of material, violating the rule of clarity and the rule against overbreadth. thus, sexual expression which is incident but not obscene is protected under freedom of expression.

Corrupt sexual expressions or overly violent and cruel expressions do need be regulated away from the minds of juveniles, but such regulation should be limited to only juveniles, Totally banning indecent materials and revoking registration of the publisher is excessive as a means for juvenile protection, and debases adults' right to know to the level of a juvenile's, violating the rule against excessive restriction.

C. Personal opinion (Cheong, Han-sae-beol)

Freedom of speech and press protects works which, taken as a whole, have serious literary, artistic, political, or scientific value, regardless of whether the government or a majority of the people agree with the ideas. But the public portrayal of obscene materials for its own sake, and for the ensuing commercial gain, is a different matter and mere indecency is a notch less offensive than obscenity. Therefore the Courts has held that indecent material is protected under freedom of speech and press. I presume that this protective purpose is constitutionally adequate.

Solicitation Ban case[37]
(기부금품모집금지법 제3조 등 위헌제청)
96Hun-ka5, May 28, 1998

A. Summary of the case

The claimant was prosecuted in the Seoul District Court on charges including a violation of the Labor Disputes Adjustment Act and solicitation of contributions without obtaining approval. They made motion for constitutional adview of the statute and the presiding court granted it. The court in this case reviewed Article 3 of PSCA(Prohibition on Soliciting Contribution Act)and found it unconstitutional.

B. Issue of the law

1) the right to pursue happiness (Article 10 of the constitution) : This fundamental right includes a general freedom of action and a right to freely develop personality. The act of soliciting contributions is protected thereunder and prohibiting on soliciting contributions is an act of restricting the right to pursue happiness.

---

37) Ibid., 156ff.

2) license by an administrative authority: The procedure of approval should not eliminate the right itself, and anyone who meets all the substantive requirements for approval should be given the right to request that the ban be lifted; however, Article 3 of PCSA leaves ultimate decision without specifying the conditions when approval shall be given.

3) limitations of basic rights: In order to minimize the extent of restriction of basic right, the legislature should first consider using the means restriction, and resort to complete ban only when it is found to be insufficient for accomplishing the targeted public interest. The purpose of this statute(property rights and stable livelihoods) can be sufficiently accomplished by a restriction on process and method of solicitation. Therefore, Article 3 and its penalty provisions in Article 11 exceed the scope necessary for accomplishment of the legislative intent in restricting basic rights.

C. Personal opinion (Park, Jin-a)

This problematic statute has clearly unconstitutional elements in itself. Everyone in democratic society have right to pursue their happiness by action of contributing to accomplish their self-realization. As constitutional court mentioned, this Article excessively restricts the fundamental right and leaves administrative body to have the ultimate decision by themselves. It means our fundamental right depends on decisions by the government case by case not based on the statute.

Automobile Driver's No-Fault Liability case[38)]
(자동차손해배상법 제3조 단서 제2호 위헌제청)
96Hun-Ka4, etc., May 28, 1998

A. Summary of the case

In this case, the Constitutional Court upheld the provisions of the Guarantee of Automobile Accident Compensation Act requiring the including free riders and guests of his courtesy, regardless of his fault.

The second proviso of Article 3 of the Guarantee of Automobile Accident Compensation Act stipulates that driver have not fault but take the consequence.

These days, Automobile is important transportation. The occurrence of an automobile accident that our don't know, who is fault. Insurance companies and business-legal scholars that the rule of no-fault liability of a driver to all passengers violates the constitution.

The claimants and complaint were liability for an this accident. They requested constitutional review of the above provision in the Constitutional Court.

---

38) Ibid., 230ff.

B. Issue of the law

In a unanimous decision, the Constitutional Court upheld the second proviso of article 3 of the Guarantee of Automobile Accident Compensation Act for as follows.

The Constitutional Court adopts the principles of social state. Passenger from traffic accident injury and damage. Driver imposed of no-fault liability that does not beach the free-market economic order.

In a relation to right to property, our country adopts the principles of social state. Driver's no-fault liability imposed minimum reasonable limitation. It does not infringe upon the driver's right to property.

In connection with equality, passenger have a danger in automobile accident. So Because driver dominates automobile, responsibility exists. Therefore, the above provision differentiating the passengers from the non-passengers and applying no-fault liability to both the driver at fault and those without has a rational basis and does not violate the principle of equality.

C. Personal opinion (Lee, Soo-jeen)

I don't agree with Constitution Court decision. Because, driver is very important in automobile. But no-fault liability for accident, driver have responsibility that too heavy responsibility. I think that liability is limited.

CASE 39

Appointment of Acting Prime Minister case[39]
(대통령과 국회의원간의 권한쟁의)
98Hun-Ra1, July 14, 1998

A. Summary of the case

When the National Assembly could not vote on ratification of Kim jong-pil as the new Prime Minister. In this case, the entire group of the opposition party members brought a competence dispute against the President, but their request was dismissed for lack of justifiability requirements.

On February 25, 1998, the respondents President Kim Dae-jung took office. And same day, appointed Kim joung-pil as the Prime Minister and sought the consent of the National Assembly on that matter. But The National Assembly was not held by Opposition party's absence from February 25March 2. Then, the 189th Extraordinary session began around the 21st minute of the 15th hour of March 2, 1998 in bipartisan presence. Supposed Prime Minister appointment motion but I was not voted.

After all, ratification of the appointment failed, the President accepted resignation from Prime Minister Ko-gun. And then, the President

39) Ibid., 183ff.

appointed Kim Jong-pil as the Acting Prime Minister.

The plaintiffs, the President infringed upon the power of the National Assembly and the plaintiffs to ratify appointment of the Prime Minister. They sought invalidation of the appointment of the Acting Prime Minister.

B. Issue of the law

The request was dismissed by the majority opinion of five justices. Justices Kim Yong-joon, As to the claims of prospective infringement, the power to review and vote concerns a legal relationship among the representatives themselves or between them and the speaker, and does not concern the relationship between the President and the representatives. His appointment is not likely to infringement upon the representatives' power.

Justices Cho Seung-hyung and Koh Joong-suk pointed out that the National Assembly can still vote on the appointment, and the plaintiffs who form the majority in there can influence the outcome of such vote and resolve the dispute thereby. There is no legally protectable interest in this case.

Another opinion is member of the National Assembly sought that can not request power dispute judgment against President or Speaker of the National Assembly.

C. Personal opinion (Lee, Soo-jeen)

I agree with Constitutional Court decision. First, the plaintiffs did not neglect the procedure. Second, the Republic of Korea with separation of power. In this case, It seems not to be judicature's power.

CASE 40

Inheritance by Default case[40)]
(민법 제1026조 제2호 위헌제청)
96Hun–Ka22, etc., August 27, 1998

A. Summary of the case

In this case, the Constitutional Court found nonconforming to the Constitution Article 1026 (ii) of the Civil Act that imputes absolute acceptance to an heir who fails to give qualified acceptance or relinquish within three months from the date of his or her knowledge of the inheritance. The claimants and complainant passed the three-month periods of consideration, not knowing the amounts of debt of the deceased not due to their own fault. They argued that the above provision violates the constitutional rights to property, pursuit of happiness, and equality, and requested constitutional review. Some motions were granted and referred to the Constitutional Court and those who were denied filed constitutional complaints.

---

40) Ibid., 232ff.

B. Issue of the law

1) Examined whether or not Article 1026 (ii) imputing absolute acceptance of the inheritance to an heir who has knowingly defaulted for three months on his or her inheritance violates property right and private autonomy. : The provision may impose all the liabilities of the deceased on the heir even when he has not acknowledged selectively or relinquished the inheritance because he, due to none of his fault, did not know that negative assets exceeded the positive ones. The provision is an exception to the constitutional principles of private autonomy and liability for fault, violating the heir's right to property and private autonomy protected by the Constitution, and is therefore un-constitutional.

2) Nonconforming to the Constitution : An unqualified decision of unconstitutionality will create a vacuum in law whereby the legal relations surrounding the inheritance cannot be established by default when the heirs are silent. Such decision will also create a confusion in law whereby even the negative assets not exceeding the positive ones cannot be imputed to the heirs who passed the period of consideration due to their own fault cannot be subject to a default rule. Also, any correction of unconstitutional provisions falls under the legislative discretion.

C. Personal opinion (Lee, Su-rim)

I agree Constitutional Court opinion. The claimants and complainant not knowing the amounts of debt of the deceased not due to their own fault. The above provision does not provide any measure of relief for such heirs and imposes all the inherited debts on the heirs regardless of their will. It is not an appropriate means of limiting basic rights.

Nevertheless this decision is, the Court strongly called for legislative revision by imposing a time limit while preventing the vacuum in law by keeping the statute effective in the meantime. It, however, is desirable for the legislature to give life to the Court's intent in fashioning the decision of nonconformity and provide relief to the claimants and complainant and to those similarly situated.

Wordlist

abdication(권력의) 포기, 기권
abide 감수하다, 인정하다, 집행하다
abolish (제도·법률 등을) 폐지하다
above provision 위 조항
abridge (권력 등을) 약화시키다
abridged ~을 단축하다, 생략하다
absolute 안전한, 무조건의, 절대적인
abstract 추상적인
abuse (지위, 권리)를 남용하다
academia 학구적인 세계, 학계
acclaim 환호하다, 갈채하여 인정하다
accomplish 이루다, 성취하다
accordance 일치, 조화, 부합
accrual 이자(의 발생), 자연증식
accrue 권리로서 발생하다
accumulate 모으다, 축적하다 ; 쌓다
accusing 비난하는, 나무라는
acknowledge (채무 등을) 승인하다
acquiesce (마지못해) 동의하다
acquisition (권리, 소유권의) 귀속
adequate (어떤 목적에) 충분한
adhere 고수하다, 집착하다, 지지하다
adjacent 접근한
adjudicate 판결을 내리다, 판결하다
adjudication 판결, 재정, 파산선고
adjust 맞추다, 조정하다
adjustment (쟁의 등의) 조정
administration (법률 등의) 시행, 집행
administrative 관리의, 경영상의
administrative guidance 행정지도
admittedly 틀림없이, 확실히
adultery 간통, 부정, 불륜 ; 간통죄
advantageous 유리한, 형편이 좋은
adverse 역의, 거스르는, 반대하는

advocate 옹호[변호, 지지]하다
advocated 옹호자, 변호사, 옹호하다
affirmative 확언적인, 긍정적인
affix 첨부하다, 붙이다, 더 쓰다
aforementioned 앞서 말한
aggregate 모으다, 집합적인
agitation 동요, 흥분 논의, 검토
aid 원조하다, 돕다, 촉진하다
alienation 양도, 이전, (예산의) 전용
allege 단언하다, 진술하다, 내세우다
allegedly 주장한 바에 의하면, 이른바
alter 바꾸다, 개조하다, 변하다
alternative 대안, 다른 방도
ambience 분위기, 현장감
ambiguity 두 가지 뜻 모호
amend (의안을)수정하다, 개정하다
amendment (헌법·법률) 수정, 개정
amidst …의 한복판에
annexation 부가, 첨가, 부록
apparatus (정치 활동 등의) 기구
appeal 항소하다, 상고(상소)하다
appellate 항소(상고)의
apply for 신청하다, 의뢰하다
appraisal 값 매김, 감정, 견적
appreciation (가격의) 등귀
appropriate 전유하다, 횡령하다
appropriateness 적정, 적합, 타당성
approval 찬성, 동의, (정식) 승인
approve 승인하다, 확인하다
approximately 가까워지다, 접근하다
arbitrarily 제멋대로,
arbitrariness 임의, 독단, 변덕
arbitrary 임의의, 자의적인, 방자한
arrest 체포하다, 검거(구속)하다

artificial 인공적인, 모조의, 꾸민
ascendancy 우세, 패권, 지배권
aside from ~을 제외하고
assassination 암살
assembly 집회, 모임, 의회, 입법부
assert (권리) 주장, 옹호하다
asserting 단언하다, 명언하다
assessment (과세를 위한) 평가, 세액
assets 자산, 유산
assign 할당하다, 배당하다; 정하다
association 연합, 교제, 협회
attached 매어져있는, 첨부한
attempted 기도한, 미수의
attorney 법률가, 변호사, 법정대리인
authoritarianism 권위주의, 독재주의
authorization 권한부여, 수권, 위임
authorizing 정당하다고 인정하는
automatically 자동적으로
autonomy 자치(권)
ban 금지, 금제, (여론의) 반대, 비난
banc 판사석
bargaining 교섭
barring ~이 없으면, ~을 제외하고는
baseless 기초(근거, 이유)가 없는
basis 기초, 기저, 토대
be secondary to ~보다 부차적이다
bearer 운반인 (수표, 어음의) 지참인
bipartisan 두 정당 파의, 초당파적인
blanket (법 등을) 포괄적으로 적용
boundary 경계(선), 끝, 한계, 한도
breach 위반, 침해, 불이행, 어기다
broad 폭이 넓은
broaden 넓히다
brotherhood 형제애, 동포애
budget 예산, 예산안
burden 무거운 짐, 부담, 걱정
cancellation (계약위반으로) 해제
candidacy 입후보
capability 능력, 재능, 수완

capitalism 자본주의(체제)
casualty 재해, 사상자
ceases 그만두다, 멈추다, 끝나다
censorship 검열
census 조사, 인구조사
certain 확실한, 확신하는
certificate 증명서, 증명; 인증, 공증
characterizing 법률관계의 성립결정
charge 고발하다, 책망하다
chill 오싹하게 하다. 열의를 꺾다.
circumstance 상황, 사태, 경우, 사정
claim 요구하다, 청구하다
claimant (배상 등의) 원고
clarity 명쾌함, 명석함
classify 기밀 등급에 따라서 나누다
clause 조항, 계약 조항, 약관
clientele 소송 의뢰인, 피보호자
coercive 강제적인, 고압적인
collateral 2차 담보, 직계가 아닌
collective action 단체 행동
collusion 공모
combine 결합시키다, 연합시키다
commencement 제정법의 효력 발생
commission 위임, 위원회
commit 잘못이나 죄를 저지르다
commitment 범행, 구속, 공약, 서약
communist 공산주의자
comparable 비교되는, 동등하게
compensation 보상, 형사보상, 보수
competence 권한, 법적 능력
complainant 원고, 고소인(plaintiff)
component 구성하는, 성분의
comprehensively 포괄적으로
compromise 타협, 화해, 양보
compulsory 강제적인, 강제하는
compute 계산(산정)하다, 평가하다
concrete 구체적인, 구상적인, 현실의
condemn 유죄 판결을 내리다
conduct 행위, 행동, 지도, 안내

confirm (진술 따위를) 확증하다
confiscate 몰수하다, 징발하다
conform (법률에) 맞게 행동하게하다
confrontation (법정 등에서의) 대결
conjugal 부부(간)의, 혼인(상)의
consensual 약정의
consequence (영향의) 중요성
consistent with 일치하는, 양립하는
consolidate (권력 등을) 강화하다
conspiracy 불법 공모, 공동 모의
conspire 공모하다, 작당하다
constitute 제정하다, 설립하다
constitutional 헌법(상)의
constitutionality 합헌성, 합법성
constrained 강제적인, 무리한
construe 해석하다, 추론하다
contention 말다툼, 논쟁, 논전; 주장
contiguous 접근하는,
contract 계약, 약정서, 청부
contradiction 부정, 부인 반박, 반대
contrarily 반대로 이에 반해서
contravene (법률을) 위반하다
contravention 반대, 위반, 경범죄
contribute 기부하다, 기증하다
contributing 기부, 기증, 기여, 공헌
controversy 논쟁, 논의, 말다툼
convict ~의 유죄를 입증하다
conviction 신념, 확신, 유죄의 판결
convincing 설득력 있는
corporation 법인
corrupt 타락한, 부패한
counterpart (한 쌍의) 한 쪽, 상대방
countervail 상쇄하다, 무효로 하다
countervailing (반대 작용으로) 무효
coup d'tat 쿠데타, 무력 정변
creativity 창조력, 창조성
creditor 채권자
customarily 습관적으로, 관례상
de facto 사실, 사실상, 사실상의

deadlock 막힘, 동점, 이중자물쇠
debase 〈품질, 가치 등을〉 떨어뜨리다
debate 토론, 토의, 논쟁
debilitate 쇠약하게 하다
debt 금전채무, 채무, 금전채무소송
decease 사망하다
declaration 선언문, 선언서, 발표
declare 신고하다, 공표하다
decree 법령, (법원의) 명령, 판결
deduce 연역하다, 추론하다
deduct 빼다, 공제하다
deduction 빼기, 공제, 삭감; 공제액
defendant 피고, 피고인
defense 변호, 답변(서)
defense industry 방위 산업체
deferred 연기된, 거치한
definitive 결정적인, 최종적인 권위
degrade 품위를 떨어뜨리다.
delegate (권한 등을) 위임하다.
delegate 대표하다 위임하다
determination 판결, 결정
delegation 대표 임명; 위임
delegation 위임, 대표 파견, 대표단
deliberation 숙고, (정식의) 심의
demand 청구, 신청, 요구
democratization 민주화
denial 부인, 부정, 거절, 거부, 자제
denote 표시하다, 나타내다
deny 부정하다, 취소하다
deposit 예금하다, 공탁하다, 맡기다
depreciate 평가절하하다
depreciation 가치 하락, 가격의 저하
deprivation 박탈, 사회적 불이익
deputy 대리(인); 보좌관, 부관 대표자
derivative 유도적인, 파생적인
derive 끌어내다, 추론하다, 획득하다
designate 명시하다
designated 지정된, 관선의
despotism 전제 정치, 전제 정부

deter 제지하다, 단념시키다, 방해하다
determination 판결
determine 결정하다, 확정하다
deterring 단념시키다
deviate 빗나가다, 일탈하다
deviation 벗어남, 탈선, 일탈
dictate 구술하다, 명령하다, 지시하다
dictatorship 절대[독재]권 독재 정권
differ ~와 다르다, 의견이 다르다
differentiate 구별 짓다
director 지도자, 지휘자, 관리자
disastrous 비참한
disclosure 발각, 적발, 발표, 공개
discolor 변색시키다, 더럽히다
discontent 불만, 불평, 불복
discourage 용기를 잃게 하는
discretion 신중, 판단, 분별, 사려
discriminate 차별 대우하다
dismiss 기각하다, 각하하다
disorderly 무질서한, 난잡한
disparity 상위, 부등, 불균형, 불일치
dispose 배치하다, 처리하다, 처분하다
dispute 논쟁, 논의, 이의 제기하다
disruption 붕괴, 혼란, 차단
dissent 이의를 말하다, 불찬성
dissenting 이의 있는, 반대 의견의
dissipation (법적 관계의) 해소
dissolve 해산하다
distortion (사실 등의) 왜곡, 곡해
distribute 분배하다, 분류하다
distribution 분배
debtor 채무자
diversion 전환 (자금의) 유용
dodge 피하다, 회피하다
domain 영토, 범위, 계.
draft 기초된, 초안의, 초벌, 밑그림
drainage 배수, 배수로, 하수구
drastically 과감하게 철저하게
due process 정당한 법의 절차

duplicate 복제하다, 모방하다
duplication 복사, 복제, 복사물
editorial 사설, 논설, 사설의, 편집의
elaborate 공들인, 정교한
eliminate 제거하다, 삭제하다
emerge 드러나다, 알려지다, 판명되다
enact 〈법률을〉 제정하다, 규정하다
enactment 입법, (법)제정 법률, 법령
encroach 침략하다, 침입하다
endeavor 노력하다, 애쓰다, 시도하다
enforcement 시행, 실시 강제, 강요
engender 생기게 하다, 발생케 하다
engulf 삼키다; 완전히 뒤덮다, 감싸다
ensuing 다음의, 뒤이은
enthusiastically 열심인, 열광적인
entrepreneurial 기업가의, 기업가적인
entrepreneurship 기업가의 임무
entrust 〈책임·임무 등을〉 맡기다
enumerate 열거하다
enumerative 계산상의, 열거하는
envisage ~을 마음에 그리다
equivalently 동등한 대등한
equivalently 상당하는, 대응하는
erosion 부식, 침식
essential 근본적인, 본질적인
essentially : 사실상
establish (법률, 제도)를 제정하다
estate 재산, 유산; 재산권, 물권
estimated 어림잡다, 견적하다
evaluate 평가하다
evaluation 평가, 판정, 견적
evasion (책임·의무 등의) 회피, 기피
evasive 파악하기 어려운, 애매한
evil (도덕적으로) 나쁜, 부도덕한
eviscerate 골자를 빼버리다
examining 증인신문, 신문, 조사
exceed (수량, 정도, 한도)초과하다
exceeding 대단한, 지나친
exceptional 예외적인; 특별한

exceptionally 예외적으로, 특별히
excess 여분의, 초과한
excessive 과도한, 과대한, 과다한
excessive restriction 과도한 제약
excessively 과도한, 지나친, 엄청난
exclusion 제외, 배제, 추방
exclusive 배타적인
executable 실행(집행)할 수 있는
execution 수행, (법의) 집행, 이행
executive 집행부(의), 행정부(의)
exempt 면제된, 면세의
exemption 면제, 공제
exhausted 고갈된, 다 써버린
exhaustion 고갈, 소모, 극도의 피로
existence 존재, 실재, 현존, 실체
expedite 방해가 없는, 급속(신속)한
expedition 신속, 기민
expiration (기간ㆍ임기 등의) 만료
expire 〈계약ㆍ보증 등이〉 만기가 되다
explicit 뚜렷한, 명백한, 명시된
expression (사상, 감정 따위)의 표현
expropriation 공용수용, 수용
extend (채무 지급을) 연기하다
extenuating 죄를 가볍게 하는
external 외부의, 외면적인
extinguish (부채 등)을 소멸시키다
extrapolate 추정하다
fabricate (문서를) 위조하다
facilitate 쉽게 하다, 촉진하다
factor 요인, 인자, 요소
faithfully 성실하게, 충실히, 정확히
fate (개인ㆍ국가의 종종 불운한)
favor 호의, 친절, 은혜
feudal 영지[봉토]의; 봉건 (제도)의
fidelity (부부간의) 정절; 충실, 성실
fine 벌금, 과료, 벌금을 과하다
flagship 기함, 제독함, 본사, 본점
forbidden 금지된, 금단의
forfeit 벌금, 과료 상실하다, 박탈하다

formally 형식적으로, 공식적으로
formulate 공식화하다
founder 창립자, 창설자
framework 뼈대, 골격 ; 구조, 구성
gear (계획, 요구 등에) 조정하다
geographically 지리학의, 지리적인
gerrymandering (부정한)선거구 개편
gist 요점, 요지, 골자
grant 양도하다, 승인하다, 허가하다
granted 승인된
grievance 고충, 불안, 불복
grievous 슬픈, 통탄할, 비통한
guarantee 보증, 보증계약, 피보증인
hail 부르다, 맞이하다, 쏟아지는
hamper 방해하다, 훼방하다
hardship 고난, 고초, 신고, 곤란
heir 상속인, 부동산 상속인
hereby 이로써, 이 문서에 의하여
hereinafter 아래에(서는), 이하에
hierarchy 권력자 집단에 의한 통치
High Court 대법원
hinder 방해하다, 저지하다
homogeneity 동종, 동질성
humanity 인류, 인간성 인간애
humiliate 굴욕감을 느끼게 하다
ignite 타오르게 하다, 흥분시키다
illustrative 설명적인, 실례가 되는
immature 미숙한, 미완성의
immense 거대한, 막대한, 광대한
immune 영향을 받지 않는, 면책한
immunity (책임ㆍ채무 등의) 면제
impair (가치, 힘, 건강 등을) 감하다
impairment 손해, 피해.
impede 방해하다, 지연시키다
impermissible 허용될 수 없는
impetus 힘, 기동력, 기세; 자극, 충동
implement 이행하다, 실행하다
implicate 관련시키다, 연좌시키다
implied 함축된, 언외의, 암시적인

import (감정 등을) 이입하다
impose (의무, 벌, 세금 등을) 과하다
imposition 부과, 세금
impracticable 실행 불가능한
imprisonment 투옥, 강제적 구속
impute (책임 등을) 돌리다, 고소하다
in comparison with 와 비교해 볼 때
incapacitate 무능력하게하다
incarceration 투옥, 감금, 유폐
incentive 격려, 자극, 장려금, 보상물
inception 처음, 시작, 발단
incident 사변, 사건
inclusion 포함, 포괄, 포섭
incorporate 법인으로 만들다
incumbency 재직[재임] 기간
incumbent 현직의, 현직자
incur 초래하다, 발생하다
indecency 저속
indecent 저속한
indefinite 불명확한, 일정하지 않은
indemnification 보상, 배상, 보장
indigent 가난한, 곤궁한
indiscriminate 무차별의, 무계획적인
indispensable 필요불가결한
inequality 불평등, 불균형, 불균등
inevitable 피할 수 없는, 부득이한
inevitably 불가피하게, 필연적으로
infringe (법률, 협정)을 위반하다
infringement (법규를) 어기다, 범하다
inherent 고유의, 본래부터의, 타고난
inherit 상속하다, 물려받다
inheritance 상속 재산, 유산
initial 처음의, 최초의, 시초의
initiate 시작하다, 개시하다, 창설하다
initiative 국민 발안, 의안 제출권
in-kind 현물 지급의
innocuous 무해한, 악의가 업는
inoperative 효력이 없는, 무효인
inseparability 불가분성

inspection 조사, 검사, 검열, 점검
installation 취임, 임명, 임명식
instance 소송(사건), 소송절차
instigate 유발하다 부추기다
instigation 선동, 교사 자극, 유인
institution (사회) 제도; 법령, 관례
insubordination 반항, 명령거부
insufficient 불충분한, 부족한
insurrection 반란, 폭동, 반역행위
integral 완전한, 필수의, 구성요소의
integrity 완전, 온전함 성실 보전
intent 의향, 목적, 의지, 계획
interfere 방해하다, 훼방하다
interpretation (법, 계약서) 해석, 설명
intervene 개입하다, 소송에 참가하다
intervention (제3자의) 소송참가
intimidate ～을 두려워하게 하다
intricately 얽히게, 복잡하게
introduce 소개하다, 안으로 들이다
invalidation 무효로 함, 무효화, 실효
invasion 침입, 침략, 침공, 침해
investigating 조사하다, 수사하다
involved (사건 등에) 깊이 관련된
irrational 불합리한, 이성이 없는
irrational 이성을 잃은
irrespective of …에 상관없이
jeopardize 위태롭게 하다
judicial 사법의, 재판의; 법관[판사]의
judicial review 사법 심사권
judiciary 사법부
junta (쿠데타 후의) 군사 정권
jurisdiction 사법(재판)권, 지배(권)
jurisprudence 법률학, 법학 이론
justice 정의, 합법성, 법관, 판사
justified 납득이 되는, 이치에 맞는
juvenile 젊은, 어린, 소년소녀를 위한
kernel 핵심, 요점
Labor Disputes Adjustment Act
          노동쟁의조정법

Labor Management Consultative
Council Act 노사협의회법
Labor Relations Commission Act
　노동위원회법
Labor Standards Act 근로기준법
lacking 부족하여, 결핍되어; 모자라는
lawful 합법적인, 적법한
lawsuit 소송, 고소
legality(legalism) 적법, 합법, 정당
legislation 법률, 제정, 입법
legislative 입법상의, 입법권을 가진
legislator 입법자, 법률 제정자
legislature 입법부의, 주 의회
legitimacy 적출, 합법성, 정통성
legitimate 합법의, 적법한
lender 대금업자
lessor 임대인, 대지인, 대가인
lest …하지 않게, …하면 안 되니까
levy (세금·기부금 등을) 징수하다
liability 경향이 있음, 빚, 책임, 의무
license 면허, 인가, 허가증
likelihood 있음 직함, 가능성, 가망
limitation 한도, 한계
link 고리, 연결된 것, 유대
Liquor Tax Act 주세법
literally 문자 그대로 정말로 실제로
litigation 소송, 기소
livelihood 살림살이, 생계(수단)
livelihood 생계, 살림
loom 어렴풋이 나타나다
Ltd. limited 유한[주식]회사
magnitude 크기
majority 대부분 과반수 다수당 성인
makeshift 임시변통의, 일시적인
malignant 악의 있는
malpractice 배임 행위, 비행
mandate (법원의) 명령, 직무집행영장
mandatory 명령의, 의무적인
manifest 명백한, 분명한, 일목요연한

manifestation 태도 표명
manipulation 교묘한 처리, 조종 조작
mar 손상시키다, 훼손하다, 망쳐놓다
martial 전쟁의, 군사의
martial law 계엄령
mature 성숙한, 숙성된, 원숙한
meantime 그동안, 동시에, 한편
measure 법안; 법령, 조례
mention 말하다, ~에 언급하다, 언급
merely 단지, 그저, 기껏
merit (청구의) 실태; (소송의) 본안
monarchy 군주 정체[정치], 군주제
monogamous 일부일처의
monopoly 전매, 독점 전매(독점)회사
mortgage 저당
motion 명령[재정] 신청; 발의; 제의
multiplicity 다수, 다양성
murder 살인, 모살; 살인 사건
mushrooming 급격히 퍼지는
mutiny 폭동[반란]을 일으키다
National Assembly 국회
nationwide 전국적인, 전국적으로
negligence (사법상의) 과실
nomination 지명, 추천
nominee 지명된 사람, 수령 명의자
nonconforming 계약에 부적합한
nonconformity 비협조, 불일치
non-intervention (내정)불간섭
normalization 표준화, 정상화, 정규화
nulla poena sine lege 죄형법정주의
nullification 무효, 파기, 취소
nullify (법적으로) 무효로 하다
nurture (아이를) 양육하다, 기르다
object to 반대하다, 항의하다
objectively 객관적으로
obligation 책무, 의무, 약정, 계약
obscene 외설한, 추잡한, 역겨운
obscenity 외설. 외설행위.
observe 준수하다, 지각하다

observing 주의 깊은, 방심하지 않는
obstruct 막다, 차단하다, 방해하다
obtain 얻다, 손에 넣다, 획득하다
offering 공물, 헌금, 신청, 제공
omission 부작위, 생략
on behalf of 남을 대신(대표)해서
opportunity 기회, 호기, 행운
opposition 반대, 야당, 반대당
optimization 최대의 활용, 최적화
ordinance 법령, 포고, 명령
ordinary 보통의, 통상의, 정규의
originate 시작하다, 일어나다
outcome 결과; 과정; 성과, 결론
outcry (대중의) 강력한 항의
outlaw 금지하다, 비 합법화하다
outline 윤곽을 그리다, 약술하다
overturn 전복, 와해, 붕괴
ownership 소유권
parallel 〈목적·경향 등이〉 서로 같은
paralyze ~을 마비시키다
parental 어버이의
partial 불완전한, 일부분의
particular 특별한, 특정한, 고유의
passage (의안 따위의) 통과, 승인,
passive 수동의, 무저항의
patience 인내, 인내심, 참을성; 끈기
patriarchal 존경할 만한, 원로의
payment 지불, 보수, 보상, 변제
penal 형(벌)을 받을 만
penalty 형, 형벌, 벌, 불리한 조건
penalty 형벌; 응보, 죄 값
pending 미결정의, 현안의; 계류 중의
permissible 허용할 수 있는, 무방한
permit 허락하다, 허가하다, 인가하다
perpetrator 가해자, 범인, 하수인
perspective 전망, 가능성, 예상
petition 탄원(서), 진정(서), 신청(서)
petitioner 청원자, (이혼소송의) 원고
phenomenon 현상, 사건; 사상

phrase 구, 말씨, 표현법,
pivotal 추측의, 중추의
plaintiff 원고 고소인
pledge 담보
plenary 정식의, 본식의
polity 정치형태, 국가, 정책, 방침
postponement 연기, 미루기
practical 실제의, 실제상의, 실용적인
practically 실제로, 실제로는; 사실상
practice 관행, 관습, 소송절차, 실무
praise 칭찬, 찬양, 숭배, 칭찬의 대상
preadjustment 사전 조정
preamble (조약, 법령 따위의) 전문
precedence 선행, 우선, 우위, 우선권
precedent 전례, (종래의) 관례; 판례
preclude 제외하다, 방해하다
precluding 일어나지 않게 하다
predecessor 전임자, 선배, 선행자
predictability 단정할 수 있게
predictable 예언할 수 있는, 당연한
preliminary 예비적인, 준비의
premise 기술사항
premonition 징후, 전조, 예감
preoccupied 몰두한, 여념이 없는
preparatory 준비 서면, 서론의
preparedness 준비, 각오
prepay 선불하다, 선납하다
prerequisite 불가결한, 선행조건
prescribe 시효에 의해 취득하다
preside 의장을 맡다, 주재하다
presidential 대통령의, 지배하는
presidential decree 대통령령
pressure 압력, 강제
presume 가정[추정]하다; 상상하다
pretext (사실과 다른) 구실, 핑계
prevail 우세하다, 유력하다
prevailing 우세한, 널리 보급되어
prevent 막다, 방해하다, 막아서
prevention 방지, 예방, 예방법

primary 주요한, 최초의, 근본적인
prison 교도소, 감옥, 감방; 금고, 감금
privilege 특권, 면제, 면책
problematic 문제의, 의문의, 미정의
procedural legitimacy 절차적 합법성
procedure 소송절차, 의회, 의사절차
proceed 소송을 제기하다, 처분하다
proceeding 소송을 제기하다
processes 과정, 소송절차, 소장
procurement 획득, 조달, 주선
progressive 〈세금 등이〉 누진적인
prohibition 금지, 금제, 금령
prohibitive 금지하는
prompt 상기시키다, 생각나게 하다
promulgate 〈법률 등을〉공표하다.
property 재산, 자산; 소유물
prosecute 기소하다, 공소하다
prosecution 기소, 소추
prosecutor 검찰관, 검사,
prospective 예상된, 장래에 발효되는
provide 주다, 준비하다, 대비하다
provincial 지방의, 시골의, 지방민의
provision 준비, 설비, 충당금, 조항
provisional 잠정의, 일시적
proviso (법령·조약 등의) 단서, 조건
prurient 음란한, 외설한
pseudo 허위의, 가짜의, 모조의
public sector laborers 공공부문노동
자들
publish 발표하다, 출판하다, 공포하다
punish 〈사람·죄를〉벌하다, 처벌하다
punishable 처벌할 만한
punishment 형벌, 처벌, 징계, 징벌
purchase 사다, 구입하다, 매수하다
purification campaign 정화계획
purport 의미, 취지, 목적, 의도
pursuant (법에) 따른, 준한, 의거한
pursue 뒤쫓다, 추구하다, 수행하다
qualify 자격을 가지다, 자격을 주다

question 질문하다, 심문하다
ratify 비준하다, 승인하다, 인가하다
rationale 이론적 설명, 근본적 이유
reaffirm 다시 확인하다
reasoned 사리에 맞는, 숙고한
reasoning 추론, 추리 추론, 논증
reckless 분별없는, 무모한
recognition 인식, 허가, 공인
record 기록하다, 적어놓다
recover (승소하여) 권리를 되찾다
reduction 축소, 삭감 저하, 하락
refer 위탁(부탁)하다, 회부하다
reflect 반사하다, 반영하다, 나타내다
reflective 반사하는, 반성하는
refusal 거절, 거부, 사퇴
refutes 논박하다, 이의를 제기하다
regain 되찾다, 회복하다; 탈환하다
regardless 무관심한, 부주의한
regime 정치제도[체제, 형태]
region 지방, 지역, 지구, 지대
registering 기재함, 등록함
registration 기재, 등기, 등록, 기명
regression 복귀, 회귀
regulate 규정하다, 통제하다
regulatory 규제의
rehabilitated 원상복구 시키다
reimbursement 상환, 변상
reinstate 회복하다
reinterpret 새로이 해석하다
relationship 관계, 관련
relevant 관련성 있는, 관련된, 적절한
relief 구제, 구조, 구원
relinquish (소유물을) 포기, 양도하다
removal 이동, 이전, 제거, 해임, 면직
render 〈평결을〉내리다
renewal 일신, 새롭게 하기
repeal (법률 등을)무효로 하다
repeatability 되풀이 하다, 반복하다
report 보고서, 판례집

represent 나타내다, 대표하다
representative 법률상의 대표자
repulsive 불쾌한, 혐오감을 일으키는
review 정밀하게 살피다.
repurchase 환매, 환매품
requirement 요구, 필요
reside 살다, 존재하다
residential 주거의, 거주에 관한
resolution (법원의) 판결
resolve 결심하다, 결정하다, 해결하다
resort 의지하다, 힘을 빌다, 호소하다
의지가 되는 사람(것); 수단, 방책
resourceful 자력이 있는
respondent 피고, 피항소(상소)인
restitution 반환, 손해배상, 회복
restoration 회복, 반
restraining order 금지 명령
restriction 제한, 한정; 구속, 속박
restructure ～을 개조하다, 개혁하다
retaliatory 보복적인, 복수심이 강한
retiree 퇴직자
retirement allowance 퇴직금
retroactive 〈법률 효력이〉 소급하는
retroactive 소급하는
reunification 재통합, 재통일
revenue 세입
review 재심하다
revision 수정판, 교정본, 개정판
revive (법적 효력을) 부활
revocable 폐지할 수 있는
revocation 취소
revoke 취소하다
ruling 지배하는, 통치하는, 유력한
rural 시골의, 지방의, 시골풍의
sabotage 고의로 파괴[방해]하다
sacrifice 희생하다, 단념하다
sanitation 공중위생, 위생설비
scheme 계획, 개요
scholar 학자, 학생, 장학생

seek 찾다, 얻으려고 하다
self-determination 자결, 자기 결정
self-realization 자아실현, 자기개발
self-serving 이기적인
sentenced 선고하다, 판결하다
sentiment 의견, 강점, 정조, 정서
separate 잘라서 떼어 놓다, 분리하다
settled 고정된, 정해진, 확립된
severe 심한.
sharpen 〈법률을〉 엄격하게 하다
significance 의미, 의의, 취지, 중대성
small-to-midsize 소형에서 중형의
sole 오직하나, 독점적인, 고독한
solidify 단결(결속)시키다, 굳어지다
sovereign 주권자, 원수, 군주, 국왕
sovereignty 주권, 통치권
specify 일일이 열거하다, 상술하다
speculation 투기
squarely 정면으로, 곧바로, 단호히
stake 경계를 표시하다, 구획하다
stall 농간, 속임수, 핑계, 바람잡이
statement (문서·구두에 의한) 진술
statute 성문율, 법령, 법규, 정관
statutorily 법정의, 법령의
statutory 법정의, 법령의[에 의한]
statutory mandate 법령
stipulate (계약서, 조항) 규정하다
stipulation 조항, 조건
strike down 때려눕히다
stringent 엄격한, 절박한, 핍박한
submission 복종, 항복, 순종
subsection 소구분으로 나누다, 세분
subsequent 뒤의, 그 이후의
subsequently 다음에, 이어서
substantial 상당한, 실재하는, 참다운
substantive 현실의, 실체법(상)의
substitute (에게) 대리를 시키다
subversion 전복, 파괴, 멸망
subvert (체제 권위)전복시키다

successor 승계인, 승계자, 후계자
sue 고소하다, 소송을 제기하다
sufficient 충분한
suit 소송, 청원, 요청
suit to ~에 적응시키다
supplementary 보충하는, 추가의
supplemented 추가된, 보충된
suppress 억압하다, 활동을 금지하다
suppression (반란 등의) 억압, 진압
suspend 〈형벌 등을〉 잠시 보류하다
suspicion 의심, 의혹, 혐의
swearing 욕설, 완전한, 대범한,
sympathize 동정하다 동감하다
synthetic 종합적인, 종합의, 합성의
systemic 전신에 영향을 주는
tact 가산, 부가, 우선순위취득
taxation (세금의) 과세액; 과세율
taxpayer 납세자
technical 법적으로[규칙상] 성립되는
tendency 경향, 풍조, 추세
tenure 신분보장, 재직기간
terminate 해고하다
the accused 피의자
the rule of clarity 명확성의 원칙
theoretical 이론상의, 학리적인
tort 불법행위
tragedy 비극적 사건, 참사, 참극
trans 횡단, 관통, 초월, 변화, 이전
transaction 번역
transfer 이전; 양도; 양도 증서
transgressors 범칙자, 위반자, 죄인
transitional 변천하는, 과도기의
transitional measure 과도기적 법안
transpose 바꾸어 놓다
treason (국가, 통치자에 대한) 반역죄
treasonous 반역의, 대역의, 국사범의
treasury 국고, 금고, 보고
trial 공판, 재판, 심리
ultimate 최후의, 최종의, 궁극의

unabashed 부끄러운
unanimous 만장일치의, 합의의
underlying 근원적인, 기초를 이루는
undermine (명성)을 몰래 손상시키다
undermining 몰래 손상시키는
underwrite -에 서명하다
unequivocal 명백한, 명확한, 솔직한
unfurl 펴다, 전개하다
unilaterally 일방적으로, 일면적으로
unqualifying 자격을 잃게 하는
unquestionably 의심할 나위 없이
unrealized 인식[의식]되지 않은
unreasonable 비합리적인, 무분별한
unrestrained 억제되지 않은
unwilling 마음 내키지 않는
upheld (결정판결 등을) 확인하다
urban-industrial 도시 산업
usurp (폭력에 의해) 점유하다
usurpation 강탈, 탈취, 권리 침해
vacuum 진공, 공백
vague (말 · 관념 · 감정 등이) 막연한
vicious 나쁜, 부도덕한, 타락한
victimize 희생시키다
violate (법률, 규칙 따위) 위반하다
violative 침해하는, 깨뜨리는
violator 위반자
void (계약, 약속 등이) 무효인
voidable 무효[취소]화 할 수 있는
vulgar 저속한, 상스러운
whereby 그것에 의하여, 그것에 따라
whereupon 그 후에, 그 결과, 그래서
wholesaler 도매업자
withdraw 소송을 취하하다
withdrawal 취소, 철회
withdrawn 회수한, 철회한
withhold 억누르다, 보류하다
worsen 악화되다
wrongdoer 범죄자, 가해자, 범인

Member of Constitution study team

Kim, Eun-ho (Team leader, college of law)

Lee, Su-rim (subeditor, college of law)

Park, Hye-ju (subeditor, college of law)

Park, Jin-a (preface, college of law)

Cheong, Han-sae-beol (college of law)

Kim Kun-young (college of law)

Lee, Hyun-ho (college of law)

Lee, Su-jeen (college of law)

Editor

Prof. Dr. iur. Park, kyu hwan

parkkh@ysu.ac.kr; lawpkh@hanmail.net

Textbook

The First Ten Years of the Korean Constitutioanl Court(1988~1998)
The Constitutioanl Court of Korea, 2001

박규환 ————————————————————————————————

▌약력

연세대학교 법학사, 법학석사
독일 Halle 대학 법학박사
연세대학교 법학연구소 전문연구원
DAAD 초청학자
대법원 재판연구관
베를린자유대학교 객원(계약)교수
 현) 법원행정처 전문심리위원
 현) 영산대학교 법과대학 조교수

Case Studies with the Constitution of the Republic of Korea

초판인쇄 | 2009년 8월 17일
초판발행 | 2009년 8월 17일

편저자 | 박규환
펴낸이 | 채종준
펴낸곳 | 한국학술정보㈜
주 소 | 경기도 파주시 교하읍 문발리 파주출판문화정보산업단지 513-5
전 화 | 031) 908-3181(대표)
팩 스 | 031) 908-3189
홈페이지 | http://www.kstudy.com
E-mail | 출판사업부 publish@kstudy.com

등 록 | 제일사 115호(2000. ....)
가 격 | 18,000원

ISBN   978-89-268-0267-0 93360(Paper Book)
        978-89-268-0268-7 98360(e-Book)

내일을여는지식 ▌은 시대와 시대의 지식을 이어 갑니다.